Guiding Light

A 50th Anniversary
Celebration

D0095684

Also by Christopher Schemering
Published by Ballantine Books

The Soap Opera Encyclopedia

Guiding Light

A 50th Anniversary Celebration

Christopher Schemering

Ballantine Books · New York

In memory of Charita Bauer

1922–1985

Story material and script excerpts are used with the permission of Procter & Gamble Productions, Inc.

Unless otherwised noted, photographs are courtesy of CBS, Inc.

"On the Set" photographs by author.

Photographs in "A Tribute to Charita Bauer" are courtesy of Michael Crawford.

Library of Congress Catalog Card Number: 86-90810

ISBN: 0-345-33931-2

Cover design by James R. Harris
Text design by Holly Johnson
Manufactured in the United States of America

BVG 01

Contents

Acknowledgments

For interviews, I would like to thank Michael Crawford, who provided wonderful photographs and anecdotes about his mother, Charita Bauer; Ellen Demming, whose warm reminiscences reactivated my childhood memories of Meta and Bert; Bridget Dobson, who's just as sassy as the characters she creates; Gail Kobe and Joe Willmore, who love to talk shop just as much as I do; Douglas Marland, who is not only a great writer but one of the nicest men in the business; Agnes Nixon, whose infectious laughter got me over my nervousness interviewing one of television's true legends; Arthur Peterson, who made the radio days come alive again; and, last but certainly not least, Lucy Rittenberg, a creative force whom I admire enormously.

Additional courtesies were extended by Catharine Heinz of The Broadcast Pioneer Library; John Behrens and his staff at CBS Audience Services; NBC Records Administration; Ed Rider of Procter & Gamble Archives; Debbie Lepsinger of Compton Advertising; Janet Storm of CBS; Rosemary Keough of Steve Reichl Associates; James Burnette of the Metro Washington Old Time Radio Club; Pete T. Rich, associate writer for *Guiding Light*; Al Rosenberg of Sterling's Magazines; Jean Wiggins of Arlington County Libraries, Va.; Anthony Jackubosky, Ann Irwin, Margaret H. Schemering, and Bobby Gillis for editorial assistance; and the entire cast and crew of *Guiding Light,* who made my week's visit fun and a stimulating working vacation.

I'm also grateful to three consultants on the project: David White, who provided valuable information on the radio days; Clayton Logan, who wrote the first draft of much of the TV synopsis; and John Kelly Genovese, historical consultant to *Soap Opera Digest*, who is a terrific stickler for accuracy. A heartfelt thank you for your suggestions, comments, and support.

Finally, thanks to the people who put this book together: Ann La Farge, editor par excellence at Ballantine Books; Audrey Wolf, my agent; Russell Roney of Saatchi and Saatchi Compton; and Steve Reichl, who believed in the project from the beginning.

Guiding Light

A 50th Anniversary
Celebration

Introduction

Soap operas are not just drama; they're little pockets of American history. So, it is indeed fitting that *Guiding Light*, the most insistently American of entertainments, is the longest-running drama in broadcasting history.

Even more amazing is that the serial, which began its broadcasting run on January 25, 1937, is also the longest-running show of any kind in theatrical history. The competition for this honor—the much-heralded runs of *The Mousetrap* (1952 to present) in London, *Meet the Press* (1947 to present), and *Lamp Unto My Feet* (1948–1979) on television, and the various Shakespearean productions over the centuries—pale in comparison to this great war-horse of the airwaves.

Through the last fifty years *Guiding Light* has broadcast a remarkable 13,000 episodes. Including its fifteen-minute, half-hour, and hour versions, the show has racked up over 4,000 hours of entertainment.

Through its doors have passed the famous: Mercedes McCambridge (the show's first leading lady), Gloria Blondell, John Hodiak, Cicely Tyson, James Earl Jones, Christopher Walken, JoBeth Williams, Blythe Danner, Kevin Bacon, and Sandy Dennis. Off screen, performers in the radio version gave birth to future stars of the television serial—the drama blossoming into a tradition and serving as a continuum to the generations of viewers growing up with the show.

As the outside world has endured war, catastrophe, social and economic revolutions, the inner world of *Guiding Light* has run alongside, quietly inspiring and entertaining, an accurate reflection of society. Inspirational in tone (with Reverend Ruthledge's reading lamp in the window serving as a guide for troubled parishioners), *Guiding Light* was also social document, set in a multiethnic community and dramatizing the lives of American immigrants striving for better lives for themselves and their children.

With the introduction of the Bauer family in 1948, the show was further able to mirror the American dream themes throughout the years. Papa Bauer was an immigrant carpenter who fled Germany for the promise of a better life in America. His son Bill, born here, was a transitional figure, struggling to make ends meet. Bill's sons, Ed and Mike, became successful professionals in the sixties. And in the seventies the slogan "Bauer Power," used backstage to characterize the family's resilience in the face of adversity, was not merely boastful: the Bauers had come to represent the American family who was "making it."

The message seemed clear: work hard, stick together, and success and happiness will follow. (And thus the "guiding light" theme stayed intact: through faith and family one can always muddle through.) Today, Papa Bauer's great-grandson Rick is out of medical school, coping with the pressures of contemporary society, and—to mirror modern ills—for a while resorted to drugs to keep afloat.

With its mixture of melodrama, social realism, familial conflict, and inspiration drama, *Guiding Light* has remained a vital serial for half a century. While other radio soaps during the thirties and forties retained their popularity through fantasy (Helen Trent had money, career, amusing friends, endless suitors, and remained at age thirty-five for twenty-seven years!), *Guiding Light* toyed in its premiere year with such non–soap opera issues as labor unions, isolationism, incest, a sadomasochistic relationship, and justifiable homicide. So popular were Reverend Ruthledge's dramatic sermons that a book collection (preceded by a synopsis of *Guiding Light*'s early storylines) sold a phenomenal 290,000 copies in the early forties.

Guiding Light soon became the only radio soap to make a successful transition to television, broadcasting on both media from 1952. (In 1956, the radio version was discontinued.) Amid the more entertaining aspects of the show, the serial was the first daytime TV series to inject social issues into the story, beginning with a cancer storyline in 1961. It was also the first show to present major black characters, with luminaries Ruby Dee and Billy Dee Williams tackling the roles.

Even after fifty years on the airwaves, *Guiding Light* shows no signs of flickering. Consistently among the top-rated soaps since its beginning, the program's commitment to tradition and its ability to adapt to the times (the "The" in "Guiding Light" dropped in 1977 in a gesture to contemporize) have served it well through the years. With its dynamic storylines and exciting characters, *Guiding Light* has recently replaced *General Hospital* as the rage on campuses across the country. And the soap has become an international hit (with Italy practically shutting down midday to watch the dubbed version called *Sentieri*)—proving that a good story knows no cultural barrier.

What follows is the story of *Guiding Light*. With affection and not without humor, one recalls Oliver Cromwell's vain instructions to Dutch artist Peter Lely. To paraphrase: use all your skill to paint a picture truly like me, but take out all the pimples and warts or I won't pay a farthing for it. But removing all the flaws from a life as full and robust as *Guiding Light* would truly be a disservice to its history.

So, in the following backstage history and story review, the warts may at times seem more prominent than the show's wonders. Cramming fifty years into a single volume, one sacrifices much of secondary story and subtext, and the melodramatic events have necessarily taken precedence over the emotional sweep, ironies, and quirks of the day-to-day narrative (to say nothing of character development and themes). But I have no doubt that viewers, with memories reawakened, will provide their own resonance, looking back to the many hours of pleasure spent with the Bauer family and friends.

On to television: Guiding Light's *logo in the fifties.*

The Backstage Saga 1

Guiding Light began, of course, with Irna Phillips. This irascible, dynamic woman was the creator of what we now call soap operas—dramatic serials affectionately nicknamed "soaps" because they were sponsored by soap manufacturers, particularly Procter & Gamble. Phillips began her career in Chicago, experimenting with the serial format in 1930 with *Painted Dreams*, a story about an Irish widow who fussed about the future of her brood. When her programs became local successes, she soon spread her wings nationally, creating dramas for the networks.

Among her first network shows was *Guiding Light*, which began broadcasting on NBC's Red radio network on January 25, 1937, and was supervised for Procter & Gamble by the Compton Advertising agency. Set in the fictional town of Five Points, near Chicago, and introduced by the organ strains of Goetzl's *Aphrodite*, *Guiding Light* told the story of the Reverend Dr. John Ruthledge and his troubled parishioners.

The early characters included Reverend Ruthledge, the "guiding light" of the community, his daughter Mary (played by Mercedes McCambridge), and his adopted son Ned (played by, among others, John Hodiak). The early story was tart and unusual, considering the popular fantasy-oriented soaps of the day, with Reverend Ruthledge castigating his melting-pot flock at any hint of racial prejudice and serving as arbiter of domestic squabbles. His home, with a reading lamp in the window, beckoned those in trouble.

On Radio: Raymond Edward Johnson and Mercedes McCambridge as Ellis Smith and Mary Ruthledge, 1937. (Billy Rose Theatre Collection/The New York Public Library at Lincoln Center.)

On Television: Charita Bauer and Lyle Sudrow as Bert and Bill Bauer, 1957.

But the troubles were not always to be found outside in the community, but inside the Ruthledge home itself. Years before, the doctor had adopted a ten-year-old boy, Ned Holden, and Dr. Ruthledge's daughter Mary fought for years against romantic feelings for her "brother." Complicating matters was the introduction of Ned's long-lost mother who had been emotionally abused for years by her ne'er-do-well husband. And down the street was the Kransky family whose life was in turmoil as daughter Rose rebelled against her parents' old-world ways by establishing a career and falling in love with her married boss.

Rose's subsequent pregnancy resulted in the issue of illegitimacy being tackled for the first time on radio drama. The character of Rose proved to be so popular that she and her family were spun off in a new soap, *Right to Happiness*, in October 1939. In that show, Rose became secretary to Doris Cameron. After several months, the *Right to Happiness* focused almost completely on Doris Cameron and her daughter Carolyn, and the two became the central figures on the show for the rest of its twenty-one-year run. The Kranskys moved back to Five Points and Rose fell into another torrid affair.

Meanwhile, *Guiding Light*'s Dr. Ruthledge continued to counsel those in trouble. So impressive were the minister's advice and homilies that over four decades later writer Agnes Nixon, who listened to the show as a child, could recite verbatim Reverend Ruthledge's timeless sentiment to those in need:

> There is a destiny that makes us brothers
> > None goes his way alone.
> All that we send into the lives of others
> > Comes back into our own.

Reverend Ruthledge's sermons, some of which stretched over an entire episode, were appropriately dramatic and surprisingly political.

In sermon after sermon, Dr. Ruthledge, a nonsectarian minister, would preach against the futility of war. With World War II looming around the bend, the good doctor sped up his attack against the military buildup: "Do you mothers and fathers realize as you hear the prayers of your boys—of your babies—that there are those who are testing chemicals to make deadly gas—to destroy that which you have brought into the world?" In another sermon, he asked, "And you, who are rearing to manhood the men of tomorrow, should instill into the plastic minds of your babies the real meaning of War. Take away the toys that represent war—the toy soldiers and the sailors, the guns and cannons, the miniature battlefields."

Reverend Ruthledge's Good Friday message was so popular with viewers that it was delivered by him and other ministers for the next thirty years. It concluded:

"And so, on this day of days, we—you and I—have only to remember the Crucifixion to know that in spite of greed and hate, of strife and struggle, of hatred and injustice, the sufferings of life—the faith of one Man still is the hope of mankind. The truth that He gave to the world—the truths and the principles which were uttered by His lips centuries ago, can be a Guiding Light to all peoples at all times."

Irna Phillips based *Guiding Light* and Reverend Ruthledge on her own background. In her unfinished, unpublished memoir *All My Worlds* (she also called it *The Woman in the Mirror*), Irna wrote that Five Points, "was very much like the neighborhoods on Clark Street, Maple Square Avenue, and on Winnemac Avenue in which I grew up. In the region lived Italian, German, Irish, Jewish, and Swedish families. It is often popular today for the younger generation to dismiss as a myth the melting pot story in American history. Those of us who grew up in the early years of this century, when cities were populated largely by first- and second-generation Americans, know the reality of the melting pot. The melting pot may not have worked for all ethnic groups, but it certainly was real.

"I never had any formal religious training, although I considered myself a Jew. However, I knew something very important was missing in my life. Like many young people I wanted to believe in something. I don't know why, but for some reason I did not turn to Judaism. At this stage in my life I was still uncommunicative and did not express my feelings to anyone. I did learn, however, of Dr. Preston Bradley and the People's Church. Each Sunday morning Dr. Bradley held services in a theatre on Wilson Avenue which was only a few blocks from my home. Doctor Bradley's church was nondenominational; people of all creeds and races were welcome. Although I don't consider myself a religious person, I have never forgotten the underlying theme of Dr. Bradley's approach to religion—the brotherhood of man. I created *The Guiding Light* with this minister and this theme in mind."

Irna Phillips

Born July 1, 1901, Chicago, Illinois
Died December 22, 1973, Chicago, Illinois

By the mid-forties, Irna Phillips had become the undisputed queen of soap opera. Her extremely popular radio creations included *The Road of Life, Right to Happiness, Woman in White, The Brighter Day*, and, of course, *The Guiding Light*. In her heyday, she was writing two million words a year (the equivalent of thirty to forty novels), which earned her approximately $300,000 a year. And it's safe to say that her work employed more people than any playwright since Shakespeare.

Her method of operation bore out her own acute observation, "I really don't think I write—I act." Each weekday at nine A.M., Irna would sit down in her Chicago living room in the same chair and at the same card table she used for decades. With the general story already charted—with the "approval" of Procter & Gamble and Compton Advertising—she would stare out the window and begin dictating dialogue to her lifelong secretary, Rose Cooperman. The lines would come spewing out with Irna not pausing to identify the speaker. It was up to Rose to deduce from Irna's ever-changing voice—now sweet and girlish, now gruff and soulful—who the character speaking was. When Rose would read back the dialogue, the secretary would further deduce from Irna's expressions and gestures stage directions that were to be incorporated into the script.

Irna's later enormous success with the television serials *As the World Turns, Another World, Days of Our Lives*, and others, did not mellow her. In fact, she never left any doubt about how she felt about the way her ideas were being executed. She ruled her empire with an iron hand, terrorizing producers, directors, actors, and executives at the Cincinnati-based Procter & Gamble Productions with long phone calls that had everybody on their toes.

Although she appeared a lonely figure to the press of the day, Irna had a full social life. According to her unfinished memoir, Irna had many romances—almost exclusively with doctors and lawyers! (Which, of course, explains her long obsession with doctors and lawyers in her serials.) At age forty-two and unmarried, she adopted two children. When asked why she

*Irna Phillips, 1937.
(Courtesy of the Broadcast
Pioneer Library.)*

never considered marriage, Irna replied, "Why would I want to get married? If I want to pick a fight, I can always call up one of the buffoons in Cincinnati!"

Irna was, to many, a destructive personality, whose motivations were often obscure, and who continually undermined the best efforts of creative people. More than one colleague interviewed for this book called her, quite simply, "a pain." But to quote Agnes Nixon, who had dinner with Irna just four nights before Irna's death: "Irna was her own best creation. She was colorful and quite a character and she knew it. She set out to do it all on her own and this was all very pre–women's lib. She made mistakes. She was also a hypochondriac, very warm-hearted, and very funny. And the stories about Irna Phillips are legion."

Why the eighteen-year-old Irna was drawn to a nonjudgmental, understanding minister at this point in her life soon becomes clear in her autobiography. Irna had fallen in love with a doctor in Dayton and became pregnant with his child. When he denied paternity, feisty Irna brought a court action against him and won. Although this was 1919, Irna was bound and determined to have the baby and raise the child on her own. Irna's child was stillborn, but she drew on this personal experience in writing the Rose Kransky story on *Guiding Light*, have Rose "follow a path I would have taken had my own baby lived."

Guiding Light was broadcast from studios in Chicago from January 1937 to October 1946. Chicago had become the mecca of the radio soaps, and only a year after *Guiding Light*'s premiere there were almost fifty serials on the air. Irna's soaps were consistently rated in the top ten, and one of her shows was usually number one. "Irna," recalled Arthur Peterson, who played Reverend Ruthledge for almost nine years, "was a tough cookie. She wanted to protect her work and she knew her clout and how to use it. It was because Irna cared about her characters. She wrote from her own experiences and the people she grew up with. This is why *Guiding Light* was so successful—it had truth."

Arthur, who was later to achieve TV fame as the hilariously senile Major on *Soap*, was only twenty-four years old when he won the lead role as Reverend Ruthledge, a man in his fifties. "I had played many older character parts before, beginning in college on stage and then on radio as Peter Hujaz on *The Story of Mary Marlin*. But getting the part on *Guiding Light* was special to me for many reasons. First, the potential steady income allowed me to get married! I was engaged for three years, so when I signed for the part I immediately called my fiancée to come to Chicago and we were married January 23, 1937, just two days before the premiere of *Guiding Light*.

"Secondly, this was a role I really believed in. There were so many escapist-type radio programs on the air at the time and *Guiding Light* was so different. It was a social documentary and an attempt at something realistic. Although there were soapy aspects in the various entanglements of the characters, the people were so real and Irna Phillips, who was Jewish, was very good at ferreting out any hint of prejudice. Dr. Ruthledge's saying 'There is a destiny that makes us brothers, none goes his way alone' was so close to me. This was something I could believe in.

"Knowing the nature of the drama and something about the character, my wife stitched the following words on a handkerchief, 'Think don't act.' I carried that handkerchief throughout the entire run of the show. Dr. Ruthledge would have many dialogues with a character Ellis Smith, who was a cynical man who only saw the inhumanity in his fellow man. I would have to match wits with Ellis, who was also known as "Mr. Nobody from Nowhere." Sometimes the scripts were very short, only five or six pages, with many pauses, which was unusual for radio. They weren't pregnant pauses; it was so the audience was able to digest the ideas, really think about what was being said and why.

"These were the war years, remember, and it was terribly important to bring comfort and solace to people who were so shaken up by events in Europe—the invasion of Poland, the fall of France. With the news breaking so fast, everybody's world revolved around the radio. Ruthledge wasn't phony, he wasn't a sentimentalist, so he brought great comfort to people—within the confines of a story. No matter how bad the news was, we never left the broadcast without leaving the the audience with a message of hope.

Guiding Light stars pitch in for Uncle Sam, 1943: Louise Fitch, Ed Prentiss, and Eloise Kummer made sure our boys overseas had plenty to read. The actors played Rose Kransky, Ned Holden, and Norma Greenman on the show. (Billy Rose Theatre Collection/The New York Public Library at Lincoln Center.)

Arthur Peterson

Born November 18, 1912, Mandan, North Dakota

Arthur began his career at the Federal Theatre in Chicago, where he played Dr. Stockman in Ibsen's *Enemy of the People*. After his nine-year stint on *Guiding Light*, Arthur and his wife, Norma Ransom, starred in one of the first situation comedies on television, *That's O'Toole* in 1949. The half-hour comedy was broadcast from Chicago on ABC and Arthur played handyman Tinker O'Toole. Afterwards, Arthur starred in many theater productions and was featured in such films as *Northside 777* and *Rollercoaster*.

Arthur Peterson, 1986.

More recently, Arthur delighted TV audiences for five years as the Major on *Soap*, a satire of daytime drama. (Wife Norma supplied the voice for Baby Wendy on the show.) In the last couple of years, Arthur and Norma have been touring in a production of *The Gin Game* and, like *Guiding Light*, are celebrating their Golden Anniversary—of their marriage and performing on stage together. In 1984, Arthur co-wrote and starred in the off-Broadway production of *Robert Frost: Fire and Ice*. The one-man show garnered rave reviews for the actor and he continued to tour in the production through 1986. Currently Arthur is artist-in-residence and theatrical consultant for The Federal Theatre Project at George Mason University in Virginia.

"Raymond Edward Johnson was the best of the Ellis Smiths. There were a few after that including Marvin Miller, who had a great voice—he later became famous as Mr. Millionaire on TV. [Marvin Miller played Michael Anthony on *The Millionaire* from 1955 to 1960. Miller was the executive secretary to an eccentric multibillionaire whose hobby it was to give away a million dollars to people he had never met.] Mercedes McCambridge, who played my daughter, was very bright and was going to a Catholic girls' school at the time. For a while, Hugh Downs was the announcer and he fit into the show wonderfully. He had a true sophistication, what I mean by that, he had a straightforward, no-nonsense approach to his work."

During the war years, Arthur went into the service and while overseas, he wrote several letters as Dr. Ruthledge (who was in the story serving as a chaplain in Europe) and asked Irna whether she wanted to use them. Irna adapted them and the letters were read on the air. It was during this time that a new character, Dr. Richard Gaylord, became the new pastor of The Little Church of Five Points. By early 1946, the setting had shifted to Chicago with new pastor Dr. Frank Tuttle and his young assistant Bill Brown.

During the early forties, *Guiding Light* had also been incorporated into *The General Mills Hour*, which included two other of Irna Phillips's soaps, *Today's Children* and *Woman in White*. (The last fifteen minutes was a program called *Hymns of All Churches*.) The characters moved back and forth freely between the three shows, while announcer Ed Prentiss served as the bridge between them. Dr. Jonathan MacNeill of *Guiding Light* could discuss cases with Dr. Paul Burton of *Today's Children*, then visit patients at Municipal Hospital, the setting of *Woman in White*. Announcer Ed would even "interview" the various characters from time to time, introducing new characters by asking the listener, "Do you wanna meet Tim Lawrence?"

Irna ran into trouble in 1946 when she was sued by Emmons Carlson, a writer who claimed that he had a hand in creating *Guiding Light*. Irna claimed that he merely wrote a few of the early scripts, and while only a handful were aired, Irna paid him for thirteen weeks' work. But Irna failed to report these wages to the government. She was advised to settle out of court for $5,000 in 1941 but refused, saying, "I wouldn't pay that lying bastard a dime." Years laters, Irna finally lost her court case and a $250,000 settlement. "Needless to say," Irna snapped, "his attorneys received two-thirds of the pie."

Charita in a radio publicity "still" for Guiding Light, *photographed in her home. No, that's not Charita's maid, it's her real-life mom, Posey.* (Courtesy of Michael Crawford.)

After the brouhaha, General Mills acted on their option and bought Irna's *The Woman in White* and *Today's Children*. Irna claimed that her salary had also dive-bombed from $300,000 a year to $43,000 or $850 a week. She and P & G switched the show to CBS radio, and *Guiding Light* was broadcast from Hollywood for the next three years. Irna had asked Arthur Peterson to continue in his role as Dr. Ruthledge, but Arthur and his wife were building a theater in Chicago and he declined the invitation. "When I told Irna that I wasn't going," Arthur said, "Irna told me, 'I'm going to kill off the character, so no one else could play it—including you!' And during the last few weeks the show was in Chicago I directed the show, finishing up a storyline that showcased Richard Kiley [later of *Man of La Mancha* fame] as a troubled juvenile."

Irna found the move to Hollywood a mistake. *Guiding Light's* ratings were not good and the other Hollywood-based radio shows were failing miserably. Arthur Peterson theorizes that the Hollywood actors might have contributed to the failure. "The audience didn't cotton to the different kind of performing and the accents. The acting was too highfalutin', showy, and the audience heard the difference. *Guiding Light* called for a straightforward, down-to-earth style of acting."

Guiding Light's production was moved to New York in 1949 and Irna took up residence in Chicago once again. The setting of the show had in the meanwhile changed to Selby Flats, a suburb of Los Angeles, as the character Ned Holden presented Reverend Ruthledge's friendship lamp to an old friend, Dr. Charles Matthews, pastor of The Church of the Good Samaritan.

The new story concerned the up-and-down marriage of Ray and Charlotte Brandon and the couple's attempts to adopt a child. It was here that the Bauer family were cleverly interwoven into the story. In July 1948, the radio audience heard Meta Bauer—who called herself Jan Carter—and on August 31, 1948, Papa Bauer was introduced, visiting Dr. Matthews to seek medical and emotional help for his ailing wife. (At first the Bauers were called the "Baum" family. Irna Phillips, for reasons unknown, changed the name after a few scripts.) Papa Bauer's other two children, Trudy and Bill, were soon introduced. As it turned out, Ray and Charlotte Brandon's adopted child, Chuckie, was the son of Meta Bauer, and the drama parlayed this turn of events into years of storyline.

Dr. Matthews left Selby Flats, and the Reverend Paul Keeler took over as pastor. Before Dr. Matthews left, he made a generous gift toward the building of a new hospital. Cedars Hospital—where much of the drama takes place today—began operations in the fall of 1949 with Dr. Reginald Parker as chief surgeon and Dr. Ross Boling and Dr. Mary Leland as staff doctors. While sisters

Rehearsing the radio show, 1951: Director Ted Corday, Charita Bauer as Bert, Jone Allison as Meta, Theo Goetz as Papa, organist Rosa Rio, and Lyle Sudrow as Bill.

Meta and Trudy fought for the romantic attentions of Dr. Ross Boling, Bill Bauer had met his future wife, Bertha Miller, and the two were married December 9, 1949 by Reverend Keller.

The drama juxtaposed Meta's appallingly complicated domestic situation with brother Bill's realistic problems with his new wife. At first, Bert was seen as an unsympathetic character, complaining constantly about the lack of creature comforts and pushing Bill in his career. So it must have pleased Bert when the Brandons moved from California and Bert and Bill moved into their swank Beverly Hills accommodations. Meanwhile, Meta had radio listeners riveted when she got custody of Chuckie, married Chuckie's natural father, put up with ex-husband Ted's abuse of her and her child, and finally shot and killed the sonovabitch.

The sensational trial of Meta brought reams of publicity to the show when Irna Phillips let the audience decide Meta's fate. The crafty Irna promised that if Meta was found guilty, Irna would write out her character as punishment. After the audience heard the trial testimony and summations, letters and telegrams started pouring into CBS with expressions of "guilty" or "innocent." The "special jury" voted acquittal by a margin of nearly one-hundred to one. More than 75,000 votes were received from all parts of the country. Meta was found not guilty for reasons of temporary insanity, and the popular character continued on the show. The ratings for the show soared.

Irna's Notes on the Meta White Trial

1. Consult lawyer. After questioning, is Meta removed to jail? Procedure?

2. Are photographs, fingerprints, etc., taken at this time or after the grand jury charges her with murder?

3. According to California law, what happens to Ted's estate, and how can we bring pressure from the estate to collect from Bill Bauer?

4. What plea can Ray Brandon make?

5. If the California law is the same as Illinois's, Meta will be held without bail.

6. The evening newspapers will have the story of the shooting, and thereafter there will be Hearst-like headlines, going back into the history of Meta, Chuckie, the Brandons, and Ted White.

7. While awaiting trial, Meta will be introduced to colorful characters in prison. It has occurred to me that a woman whose husband had left her and who resorted to stealing to support her children might be a pushover.

8. The adopting of a child by Ray and Charlotte. (I feel it is highly necessary during this period to show a normal, happy home. Check?)

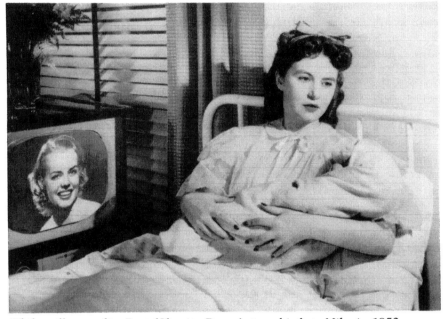

*While still on radio, Bert (Charita Bauer) gave birth to Mike in 1952.
Husband Bill was having an affair with TV star Gloria LaRue (Anne
Burr). This is another staged "still" for the fan magazines, whose readers
were starved for visuals to go along with the voices of their favorites. If
you look closely enough, you'll see that that's a plastic doll Charita is
holding.* (Courtesy of Michael Crawford.)

A month before the show began broadcasting on television in 1952, *Guiding Light* was still using radio techniques that would have been laughable on television. The announcer still played an important role, often butting into the drama, commenting, "You're about to say something to Bertha, aren't you, Bill? This habit of hers of attempting to direct other peoples lives can be a destructive one. I wouldn't want to be in your shoes, not for anything—because—well, we'll learn about this in a moment."

Even the announcer's tease at the end of the program would have to be cut for television: "Dr. Mary Leland finds herself not professionally but personally involved in the life of her patient Michael Cellini in the next dramatic episode of *The Guiding Light* brought to you by new Duz. This is Clayton Collier wishing you good day and good Duz-zing!"

Television. It had everyone worried—except Irna Phillips. Although Irna's first TV foray, *These Are My Children*, based on her popular radio serial *Today's Children*, was a big flop in 1949 on NBC, the writer was determined to make serials work in the new medium. Roy Winsor had already successfully created two new serials for television in 1951, *Search for Tomorrow* and *Love of Life*. But Irna had a major problem transferring *Guiding Light* to the medium. Would the actual faces and demeanor of Bill, Bert, and Meta fulfill the expectations—the fantasies—of the radio audience? In communication after communication, executives asked Irna whether women at home would actually take the time to sit and watch.

After viewing the two TV pilots Irna had produced with her own money, Procter & Gamble finally decided to give TV another shot, replacing its own *First Hundred Years* with *Guiding Light* on June 30, 1952. *Guiding Light*

Guiding Light *goes to television, 1952. Backstage left to right: director Ted Corday, then associate producer Lucy Rittenberg, producer David Lesan, and an unidentified representative from the Compton Advertising Agency.*

From *Guiding Light*'s television pilot experiment,
1951

Meta: I've *got* to get away. Being *here* and—*alone.*
        I—can't stand it.

Bill: (CUT TO THREE SHOT) I know what you mean,
        Meta. Sometimes, getting away can become the
        most important thing in the world. (HE TURNS
        TO BERT.) Why don't you go with her, Bert.

Bert: (CUT TO TWO SHOT) You—you're trying to get
        rid of me!

Bill: Maybe—if you get away—get a new
        perspective—

Bert: The divorce laws are easy in Mexico. *That's*
        what you're thinking—isn't it?

Bill: I didn't say—

Bert: You're ordering me out of your—out of your
        house! (BERT BREAKS INTO TEARS)

Bill: That's right—*cry.* The tyranny of tears.
        Time was when that technique moved me.

Bert: Ohhh! You're cruel, Bill Bauer! (BERT STARTS
        TO RUN FROM THE ROOM. SHE STOPS IN ARCHWAY TO
        SHOUT BACK AT HIM.) *Cruel!*

Bill: Then—maybe you can get it on a charge of
        cruelty!

producer Lucy Rittenberg remembers that early period of uncertainty: "We were in a sink-or-swim situation when I became producer. No one really knew how to put out a live fifteen-minute TV show every day. The timing of it, the logistics. I don't think there was another woman producer in television at the time. We had a meeting with the P & G brass with Irna Phillips and her sidekick, Rose. Irna turned to me and said, 'I'm very fond of you Lucy, but I can't work with women.' But as it turned out, we had one of the better working relationships that she had with anyone.

"It was a period of tremendous growth for me, as it was for Aggie [Agnes Nixon, who served as associate writer for the show]. The mistake other women made with Irna was to compete with her. And who was I to compete with Irna Phillips? We argued constantly about everything—those endless phone calls!— and Irna tried to produce and direct from Chicago. But Irna appreciated my stage background and the theatrical feel that I was trying to bring to the show. Irna was a constant irritant, but she knew what she was doing. I learned a great deal on how to tell a story—which basically has not changed over the ages.

"Irna was always threatening to take a vacation for a couple of weeks and finally did. It was great—no crazy phone calls. And Agnes did a terrific job filling in, as did Bill Bell on *As the World Turns*. Irna came back and said quietly, 'Well, I was wrong.' And I thought: wow, what an admission! Then Irna continued, 'I should never let those two take over. Everything was wrong!'

"To illustrate how contrary Irna could be: In 1953, CBS chose *Guiding Light* to be the first daytime show to experiment with a color broadcast. Everybody was terrifically excited, that is, except Irna. She got terribly nervous when something was out of her control. So the big day arrived—and what do you know?—Irna's script called for the show to take place entirely in a hospital room! Gray-white walls! White beds and uniforms! It was a disaster. And, of course, it was a long time before we got color again." (The more amenable *Search for Tomorrow* and *Love of Life*, on the other hand, were broadcast occasionally in color starting in 1954.)

With Ted Corday at the directing helm, the show began to fall into place. While other early soaps used backdrops to suggest walls and suspended doorframes and paintings by wire to suggest rooms, *Guiding Light* opted for realistic sets from the very beginning. They were underfurnished, but they were real sets. The actors wore their own clothes for a few years until Orbachs stepped in and clothed the performers for a credit on the "crawl" (the rolling list of performing and production credits) at the end of the show. The actresses did their own hair and fought over the one makeup person. But the show flourished, even under these battlefield conditions.

"The show was broadcast from Liederkranz Hall, Studio 54," remembered Ellen Demming, who played Meta Bauer. "*Captain Kangaroo* was broadcasting from there, too. There was this huge marble staircase. You went up and down the stairs with kangaroos and seals and monkeys. But they never got really chummy with you." (Actress Jada Rowland, who worked in the same building on *The Secret Storm* was not so lucky: "A llama once spat at me and an elephant ate my purse!") "The animals were all over the place," Ellen continued, "it's all quite bizarre thinking about it today, but at the time we never gave it another thought."

The stagehands had it the worst at Liederkranz. There were no elevators to move furniture and scenery through the building so everything had to be carried on the workers' backs up that huge staircase. Not only did they have to contend with the physical strain, they also had to avoid stepping into the "presents" the animals sometimes left behind on the stairs. "We argued constantly about which department would be in charge of the shit," said one stage-

Lights, Camera . . .

hand, thirty years later. "So a bunch of us got together and every time we would spot a pile, we would yell, 'PROPS!'"

Meanwhile, the radio version continued concurrently with the TV show—all the way up to 1956. "it was a very busy day," Ellen remembered, "We'd rehearse the show all morning long, then we'd be on the air at 12:45 to 1:00 P.M. for television. Then we had about forty-five minutes to get down to the radio studio on 52nd Street and we worked there until 4 o'clock in the afternoon. Then you'd go home and learn your lines. And the next morning you'd start all over again. In high school, I had worked in the early experimental days of TV [on the GE station in Schenectady], but I was not a radio person. I remember the first few times doing the radio show I hung on that music stand for dear life, just hung on in sheer panic. Because I was in the company of all these actors who had grown up on radio and knew the ropes."

With the growing importance of television, the radio shows were no longer presented live but taped the day before. In this way, the radio show served as

Action.

a rehearsal for the next day's TV show. Radio soaps were dying out in the mid-fifties—everybody wanted a piece of the action on television—and *Guiding Light*'s last radio show was broadcast in August 1956. (*Guiding Light* went out with a bang on radio: It was the number-one-rated radio soap among the nineteen network serials still on the air. By the end of 1960, the radio soaps had vanished as Ma Perkins bid a bittersweet farewell that November: "Goodbye, and may God bless you.")

On television, the religious implications of the show's "guiding light" were phased out, and the title and theme were reinterpreted to mean the support that a close family brings to romantic and domestic crises. Papa Bauer replaced the various ministers as the source of understanding and sage advice. The core characters at the beginning of the TV show were the Bauer family and Meta's new family: Joe Roberts, his young son, and his troublesome daughter Kathy, who resented Meta's marriage to her father.

Unlike *Search for Tomorrow* and *Love of Life*, two soaps specifically designed for television, *Guiding Light* was far more realistic in its storytelling. The two former shows concentrated on young heroines, flawless in moral character, who were constantly placed in a maelstrom of weak suitors, evil relatives, mob figures, and a continuous bevy of bizarre hussies who usually met their fate in a conflagration rivaling a *Dynasty* season finale. *Guiding Light* zeroed in on far less escapist fare.

Bill Bauer's struggle for success—fulfilling his immigrant parents' hopes and dreams—was juxtaposed against teenage Kathy Roberts—Meta's step-daughter—succumbing to the new freedom so popular to youths after the war. In the second half of the 1950s, the show again effectively contrasted lifestyles, concentrating on the social and professional conflicts of two brilliant physicians, wealthy Dick Grant and indigent Paul Fletcher, whose backgrounds and attitudes could not have been more different.

Early on, it was decided that the devil-may-care Meta would learn from her mistakes and change her ways. (In this way, troubled young Kathy could take center stage as anti-heroine.) Part of the transformation was "aging" the character. Ellen Demming, who was cast in the part in January 1953, remembered the transition: "Ted Corday, the director, thought I was too young for the role, and I was. The lady was supposed to be about forty and I was twenty-nine. They had my hair swept up into a chignon and they grayed the temples—for years. It looked strange and hilarious, but I guess it worked. Charita called them "little white wings." They painted the hair at my temples clown white, then I'd meet my husband for dinner after the show and he'd be mortified to be seen with this lady with white hair."

Ellen Demming as Meta, in her "little white wings," and Charita, 1954. Most of the soap characters in the fifties smoked. Today, after the Surgeon General's report on cigarette smoking, only the occasional bad guy or villainess is permitted to smoke.

"We were all very close in those days," said Ellen. "We were all very aware of another's idosyncrasies, as people are when they work closely together. But we were very fond of each other—we were a family. We saw each other socially and went to Jones Beach and had cookouts and played baseball. Charita and I were extremely close friends and saw each other hour after hour. We always shared a dressing room. And Charita and I were always looking after Theo [Papa Bauer], making sure Theo and his wife Rhea kept busy during the holidays."

There were also some fun times on the live shows. "One thing I shall never forget was the Thanksgiving show," Ellen laughed, "and Bert and Meta were in the kitchen cooking dinner. We were talking it up about how wonderful the turkey smelled and how terrific it looked. And everybody kept popping in to smack their lips. And Bert and I were to get it out and then present it to the family. Well, we went to the oven and there was no turkey!

"The prop man had forgotten to put it in. It was there in dress rehearsal. I don't know what happened to it. There was one person in the crew who always ate what Meta and Bert prepared on the show. But that was when we were off the air! Maybe he got mixed up and ate early, I don't know. Anyway, when we saw that there was no turkey we slammed the oven door shut as quickly as possible. Was the control booth and the nation ever surprised when Bert said, "I think it needs a few more minutes!"

"Another Thanksgiving," Ellen continued, "We were seated around the

In 1957, Papa Bauer celebrated his sixty-fifth birthday. Viewers sent in 40,000 letters and cards in celebration. Actor Theo Goetz reveled in them in the CBS mailroom.

table passing food around and every time a dish went past Theo [Papa Bauer], his head got in the way of the camera. In rehearsal, Ted Corday, our director, said over the speaker, "Theo, we've got to do something about this." Ted came out to the floor and looked through the camera. Finally Ted decided that every time the camera came around, poor old Theo would have to slide under the table!

"It was so hard to keep a straight face watching old Papa Bauer gradually slide under the table until he's disappear. Then he'd rise up again. It was the most awful thing and we could not stop laughing and shaking all over. Ted was furious. He kept yelling, 'It's not funny, it's not funny!' And the more angry he got the more impossible it was to get through that scene. On the air we were just as bad. Sometimes you'd get the overwhelming urge to laugh and you'd have to cut yourself with your nails to stop."

Ellen, Charita, and Susan Douglas were the leading ladies of the fifties. Because Charita, who was to play her character for an unprecedented thirty-five years, was afraid that she might call her son in the show by her own son's name Michael, she asked Irna Phillips if the child that Bert gave birth to could be called Michael also. Irna agreed and the young actor cast later on the TV show as Michael was Glenn Walken. For many years it was thought that Glenn had later changed his name to Christopher Walken, the actor who won an Oscar for *The Deer Hunter*. Actually, Glenn and Christopher are brothers. But that does not mean that Christopher Walken is not one of *Guiding Light*'s alumni: Chris filled in for Glenn from time to time on the show during the fifties.

Susan Douglas, who played troublesome Kathy, also had her share of problems on the set. "Susan was pregnant at a time when we could absolutely not have Kathy pregnant for storyline reasons," Lucy Rittenberg remembered. "We shot her up high for several months. But there were some scenes at Liederkranz Hall when she was coming down the stairs and Ted Corday would yell, 'Hold in your stomach! Hold in your stomach!' Ted was a very dear man but he often did not catch up to the reality of a situation."

When the popular Kathy was killed off in a particularly grotesque auto accident—confined to a wheelchair she was knocked over by some kids on bicycles into oncoming traffic!—CBS was deluged with torrents of angry mail. Irna sent out a form letter to those who had complained. "It was an 'Irna letter.'" said an insider, "It was phony as hell but very, very effective. It was Irna's bon voyage to the show—she was leaving to work full time on *As the World Turns*. It was all quite deliberate. And she dumped the entire mess into Agnes Nixon's lap."

Irna's Letter to the Nation

On the Occasion of Kathy Holden's Death, 1958

We are indeed interested in any comment you may have regarding the progress of *The Guiding Light.* You have recently questioned the death of Kathy Holden, and we believe there is no one more qualified to answer your question than the writer:

"We would be most unrealistic if we failed to recognize that as there is birth there is also death; as there is happiness there is also sorrow. We would be most unrealistic, lacking in integrity and honesty, if we did not fulfill what we believe is our obligation to you, the viewer.

"You have only to look around you, read your daily papers, to realize that we cannot, any of us, live with life alone. There are times when we must face the loss of a loved one. Illness, accidents, tragedy, death, exist side by side with the wonderful experience of living—love, marriage, family, birth.

"These are all part of the great pattern woven and interwoven until we see the colorful tapestry of life itself, with its lights and shawdows, its beginning and its end. We are not weavers of fairy tales.

"We hope you will continue to watch *The Guiding Light* so that you may see reflected the wonderful moments there are in living as well as the tragic."

Agnes Nixon began work as associate writer for the show in 1953 and became headwriter upon Irna's departure in 1958. Agnes signed a seven-year contract, then signed another contract for a year, which kept her as headwriter through 1966. The year before, she was named headwriter of P & G's *Another World* and wrote both shows simultaneously for a year.

After keeping *Guiding Light* at number one or number two in the ratings throughout her tenure and then rescuing the ailing *Another World*, Agnes created her own shows for ABC, *All My Children* and *One Life to Live*, where she

Guiding Light's *Christmas party, 1958. Top row, from left to right: Kay Campbell (who played Helene Benedict), Lin Pierson (Alice Holden), Zina Bethune (Robin), Whitfield Connor (Mark Holden), Louise Platt (Ruth Holden), Bernard Grant (Dr. Paul Fletcher), Theo Goetz (Papa), and Charita Bauer (Bert). Bottom row: producer Erwin Nicholson, director Jack Wood, James Lipton (Dr. Dick Grant), Joan Gray (Anne Fletcher), production assistant Peter Andrews, and Lynne Rogers (Marie Grant).*

revolutionized daytime drama with a heady mixture of social issues, high comedy, and ethnic characters.

But it was on *Guiding Light* that Agnes began her much heralded "relevance" campaign. In the 1961–62 season, Agnes decided to do a story about uterine cancer using the character Bert Bauer as the launching pad for her

Who's Afraid of Virginia
Woolf?, *1958-style. Long-
suffering Bert (Charita
Bauer) had to put up with
continual antics of alcoholic
Bill (Lyle Sudrow).*

message. The edifying storyline brought a flood of mail from appreciative
women all across the country and resulted in *Guiding Light* taking other
chances in the future.

"When I was writing Bert," Agnes recalled, "I tried to make her Everywoman in the sense that every woman could see a part of herself in Bert. Now
Bert sometimes went overboard in butting into her children's lives, but she
always meant well. Papa Bauer used to say, 'Bertha, liebling, you shouldn't get
involved, you should leave them alone.' People didn't dislike her. The audience
wrote in letters, 'God, Bert, why don't you leave it alone?' So when women
watched Bert, they might have said to themselves, 'there but for the grace of
God go I.'

"Bert was the perfect ostrich, the perfect prototype of the woman who
does not go to an obstetrician after her last baby is born. And I thought Charita,
herself, was the perfect actress to carry this message. We did the story in stages.
When Paul Fletcher learned that Bert hadn't had a physical since Ed was born,

he suggested that she come in for a complete examination. Bert was like so many women: I'm healthy, nothing can happen to me. I'm invulnerable.

"But she went ahead with the examination—I remember this scene so well because I had to write the scene six months before it actually happened to get it past the censors. Dr. Fletcher said we're going to do a Pap smear test and Bert asked, what is that? He explained in detail, and later told her she had irregular cells. Eventually, Bert had the surgery which saved her life.

"We got letters from all over. A few said that their own checkups had saved their lives. My own obstetrician said he had a half dozen patients he hadn't seen in years. He asked why they came back. And it was because of *Guiding Light*. I was surprised by the strong audience reaction, but it probably was a shock to a few executives at P & G. They were very much against doing this story. And so was CBS."

Before she left the show, Agnes introduced the first major black character

Agnes Nixon was headwriter of the show from 1958 to 1966. Today, she's the most influential force in contemporary daytime drama.

in daytime drama, nurse Martha Frazier, and subsequent writers wrote in other black characters. (Martha was played by Ruby Dee and Cicely Tyson; Martha's husband, Dr. Jim Frazier, was played by Billy Dee Williams and James Earl Jones.) Again the mostly positive audience reaction surprised the production office. "There were a few letters along the line of 'We know what you're trying to do,'" recalled producer Lucy Rittenberg. "But it certainly did not affect the ratings in any way."

It is Agnes's belief that social issues have to be well integrated in the overall story to be successful. "So Bert's cancer story wasn't an isolated incident; it served to bring Mike Bauer, who was in Venezuela, back home and be reconciled with his mother." And a light touch now and then doesn't hurt either: "I don't believe we could have made the various issues palatable to the viewers back then without a certain amount of humor. I think the humor made the people very real, believable, and lifelike to the audience. And therefore it follows that the social issues were accepted as real and believable and lifelike, making viewers think 'something like that can happen to me.'"

But Agnes's long tenure as headwriter was not all about educating the masses, even though with Bill Bauer she was able to explore the issue of alcoholism, with Paul Fletcher she introduced the idea of health care for the needy, and with Jane Fletcher she was able to tell an unusual women's lib story. (Jane lived her life through her brother, but came to terms with herself and the mistakes she had made. Jane found fulfillment through marriage and children—an appropriate choice for this particular woman.)

Although the spotlight was kept on the Bauer family, Agnes Nixon created such colorful characters as the hypnotizing, Svengali-like Alex Bowden (whom she really wanted to name Alex Mesmer!) and strong romantic heroes like Joe Turino, played by Joseph Campanella. (Agnes named Joe Turino after her housekeeper, Janette Turino.)

"Alex was so sure of himself, very worldly, very sophisticated and knowing exactly what he wanted," Agnes recalled. "He wanted to control, dominate. Yes, he did have a fondness for teenage girls. But he really did love Robin and he wasn't a dirty old man. Joseph Campanella was just terrific, so strong and masculine. I also like the Michael-Julie story very much. And I loved Paul Fletcher and Anne—Anne was played by Elizabeth Hubbard for a year and she was wonderful.

"But the one performance that really holds a particular resonance for me was when Bill came home and said he lost his job—that was the last straw for Bert. And Charita took hold of that entire complex, humiliating situation and

The Bauer family elders, 1966. Clockwise: Charita Bauer as Bert, Ed Bryce as Bill, Ellen Demming as Meta, and Theo Goetz as Papa.

what I was trying to do and just played it. It was so real. She seemed to be quietly acting out the frustrations of thousands of women and yet at the same time her heart went out to Bill. That's why I say I saw her as Everywoman. Without Charita it wouldn't have had the impact it did."

Through her thirteen years with the show, Agnes found herself continually juggling her professional career with her domestic duties. "For years," she recalled, "I did all the long-term story, the outlines, and the daily scripts. But TV was a cottage industry then. You didn't have to be in New York all the time. You'd only have be there maybe once every two months. Of course, there was constant communication over the phone, through the mail. And the show back then was still in its fifteen-minute format. But when I started doing *Another World*, I began to seek help. I had domestic help before that, but never nannies. I raised my own children. But I had to give up a lot in terms of a social life. Of course the business has really changed. You just couldn't do it today."

Agnes's children knew she worked, but the "bacon" she brought home was often in the form of "perks"—Procter & Gamble soap products. "P & G used to send huge packages of their products—Duz, Ivory, Zest, Duncan Hines cake mix. Listen, I was very grateful to them, my having four little children and not having to schlep out to the store and get all that soap powder and stuff. And my oldest daughter Cathy—she was six—used to say, 'My daddy bought me a new dress, my daddy bought me that.' My mother, who was pretty much a feminist, asked Cathy once, 'Your mother works too, doesn't she buy you anything?' And Cathy responded, 'Oh mommy just gets paid in Ivory flakes!'"

"Agnes and I worked very closely together," said producer Lucy Rittenberg, "and after we got over an early bumpy period—some executives complained that Agnes wasn't an Irna and I said 'thank God!'—it is one of my really happy memories of the show because Agnes and I were soon left to our own devices. After Ted Corday left as director to work on *As the World Turns*, Walter Gorman [who was married to soap actress Virginia Dwyer] took over, and he began a new era for the show. Before, the staging was very preset, rigid—and Irna's scripts were sacred. Walter 'opened up' the show, he brought a loose quality and a theatrical feel to the drama. He gave the actors the freedom to move out of character motivation, so there was a spontaneity and a reality which had not existed before. He had enormous respect for Agnes's writing and he would realize all the possibilities in the material. And I think he was the finest director ever in daytime."

But Walter was quite the taskmaster on the set and wasn't always tactful with the actors. A 1966 behind-the-scenes tape, provided by Procter & Gamble, amusingly confirmed this. Walter was directing Lynne Adams and Bob Gentry, who played Leslie Jackson and Ed Bauer. In rehearsing a scene in which Leslie was fed up with Ed's stringing her along, a placating Ed kissed Leslie on the nape of the neck, and actress Lynne Adams—who was wearing the hugest hair rollers known to man—couldn't help smiling. "Cut the grin," Walter roared. "You're not flattered by his approach, honey. You're not a kitten—you're a grown-up cat. Goddam it, give it some oomph. Push him away!"

When Lynne tapped Bob on the chest, Walter groaned, "Oh don't be so goddam delicate!" Lynne asked, "You want me to really *shove* him? I can't imagine shoving him." Walter answered, "Shove him! This is not detente, you're giving him an ultimatum—you want to get married, you don't want to continue in a stupid relationship that isn't going anywhere. This is the crux of the scene." Lynne agreed and gave Bob a shove that sent him flying. "Bob, Bob," Walter groaned, "What kind of a reaction is that? You could be shocked, then maybe *interested*. Haven't you ever gone with a woman and you're not interested until she slaps your face?" Bob, smiling, answered, "No." The entire crew burst out laughing.

Right before the live broadcast, Walter sat down with the actors and very gently went over some acting notes with his performers. As he walked away, the actors in unison cried, "Thank you, Walter." Curmudgeon Walter turned around and said, "You ought to thank me!" Then he stalked off to the control booth. The show was a gem, full of verve and exciting camera work, right from the moody Peggy Lee record ironically underscoring Leslie's ultimatum, to the

Well, have you ever tried blowing out candles and saying "cheese" at the same time? Guiding Light's *stars celebrated the show's fifteenth year on television, 1967. From left to right: Erik Howell, Lynne Adams, Fran Myers, and Don Scardino. Don was leaving his role as Johnny Fletcher; Erik was about to take over for him.*

end in which Leslie, out of frustration, threw a pillow directly into the camera's lens in a very arty blackout to conclude the program.

Walter had his mischievous side, too. Charita Bauer told an interviewer, "Once, we were doing a live broadcast when Walter was directing. I had a scene at the kitchen table with Papa Bauer, and once I got my cue we began the scene. Well, we were a couple minutes into the act, when somebody pressed a button in the control room, and I heard Walter *swearing* at us! Theo began rolling his eyes and mumbling, 'Vat is dis? Vat is dis?' I raised my voice and talked louder, trying to drown out the obscenities which were being heard all across America. Finally, Walter and the others began hooting with laughter. He said over the intercom, 'Charita, I knew nothing could ever stop *you*. We've been pre-empted!' Well, I was a basket case. It took ten years off my life."

After Agnes Nixon's departure as headwriter, *Guiding Light* seemed to go through a spin although the ratings remained high. Over the next two years, the show went through six headwriting regimes: David Lesan and Julian Funt, Theodore and Mathilde Ferro, actor John Boruff (who had played Henry Benedict), actor James Lipton (who had played Dr. Dick Grant), Gabrielle Upton, and Jane and Ira Avery. It was during this period that the setting of the show miraculously changed from Los Angeles and its environs to the fictional Springfield, USA.

Irna Phillips briefly came back to the show during this revolving-door period. Irna the Terrible made the very unpopular decision to kill off Robin Fletcher in a freak car accident—just as she had done nine years earlier with Robin's mother, Kathy! "When Irna came back aboard, I was very unhappy," producer Lucy Rittenberg recalled. "I was no longer the learning youngster I had been and I was not about to put up with her shenanigans. The notorious phone calls started all over again, but this time they were collect! I refused to take them and Irna was furious. But that solved the problem. We didn't have to talk anymore, and this time P & G supported me." Irna returned to *As the World Turns* shortly afterwards.

The show began broadcasting in color March 13, 1967 and expanded from fifteen minutes to a half-hour format on September 9, 1968. *Guiding Light* also discontinued its live broadcast, videotaping instead usually a day before for the next airing. (Today, it tapes a week before air show.) *Guiding Light* and *Search for Tomorrow* were the last of the fifteen-minute TV soaps and the expansion had everyone a little on edge. "When I first heard we were going to be a half-hour show," Lucy Rittenberg recalled, "my back went out. I was in a hospital bed for three weeks, editing scripts, making phone calls, and negotiating contracts. I was so happy not to be on the set!"

The opening sequence of the half-hour version was the dramatization of a heart transplant—a first for television. "There was extensive research done by our writers Jane and Ira Avery," Lucy continued. "We were loaned a machine, and the whole studio was set up like a huge hospital arena with a viewing booth for the other doctors. We had medical advisors on the set and professional nurses working as extras during the surgery." Apparently, the hubbub at the studio didn't bother Ed Bryce, who played Bill Bauer, the heart patient. After the taping was finished, the director told Ed he could finally get off the operating table. Ed didn't stir—he had fallen asleep!

The next headwriters, the husband and wife team Robert Soderberg and Edith Sommer, wrote out Bill Bauer, who had been the heart transplant patient the year before. The Soderbergs developed a story, begun by previous writers, about Ed and Mike Bauer fighting over Leslie—a complex plotline which ran for years and was extremely popular with viewers. It was the era of the birth of the fan magazines, and reporters fell over one another interviewing the *Guiding Light*'s very popular young stars, Don Stewart, Mart Hulswit, Lynne Adams, and Fran Myers.

In 1972, there was a series of tragedies for the cast and crew of *Guiding Light*. First, actor Ed Zimmermann, who played Dr. Joe Werner, suffered a heart attack on stage during a play out of town and died shortly afterwards. Just months before, Ed had published a comic novel about the backstage shenanigans of a soap opera called *Love in the Afternoon*. In the novel, there was a thinly disguised character based on "gruff" director Walter Gorman, who was adored by everybody. Only weeks after Ed's death, Walter also died of a heart attack.

Six months later, Theo Goetz, who played Papa Bauer for almost a quarter of a century, died in his sleep. In tribute to his memory, the part was not recast. The character died along with Theo and the show staged an elaborate, loving memorial to Papa Bauer. The "guiding light" mantle was passed along to Charita Bauer, whose Bert had mellowed over the years and now became the voice of reason and reassurance for the family.

By the mid-seventies, daytime television was changing. Agnes Nixon's young love stories and issue-oriented drama were pulling in huge ratings for *All My Children*; and Bill Bell's *Young and the Restless*, which featured long discussions of sex as well as actors in various states of undress, had taken off like a rocket. Although all the Procter & Gamble serials—*As the World Turns, Search for Tomorrow, Another World, The Edge of Night*, and *Guiding Light*—were doing well in the ratings race, the shows were often—and, in most cases, unfairly—criticized for being ultraconservative, slow moving, and overly bland.

Theo Goetz

Born December 14, 1894, Vienna, Austria
Died December 29, 1972, New York, New York

Before joining the cast of *Guiding Light* in 1949, Theo had been a leading
performer of the State Theater of Vienna. He served with the Austrian army
during World War I, was captured by the Russians, and spent time in a
Siberian prisoner-of-war camp. Just before the outbreak of World War II,
Theo managed to catch the last Italian ship to the United States before
Mussolini declared war. Once in America, he quickly learned English,
married painter Rhea Brown, and resumed his acting career, this time on
radio. He joined *Guiding Light* when it was on radio and continued with the
show when it made the transition to television.

Theo Goetz.

Although Theo played Papa Bauer for almost twenty-five years, he found work outside the show, appearing on Broadway in *Swan Song* and on prime-time television in *Studio One, The Philco Playhouse*, and *The Play of the Week*. But Theo would be ever identified with his role as Papa, and when the show announced that Papa would be celebrating his sixty-fifth birthday, 40,000 letters and telegrams poured into the CBS mailroom. Theo admitted he burst into tears when he saw all the congratulatory letters and presents. A P & G executive said later, "Theo didn't realize how much people loved him. He was extremely moved by this outpouring. He saw himself as a nobody who had come to this country, learned the language, and did his work. He was a very humble man and when all these thousands of people he didn't know wished him well, he was so honored."

On February 27, 1973 *Guiding Light* presented a memorial service for Papa, and the sentiment expressed was no doubt about Theo Goetz too: "Papa came to this country from another land, another country. When he was young he loved his native land, but terrible things began to happen there. And so he found his way to *this* country. And a passionate love for this, his adopted country, began to grow inside of him. He made it *his* country; its history, his history.

"He would never let us call him a wise man. He would only say that if you live a long time, you live so much that you begin to have an understanding of human events—but no more than that. He believed in people, in the basic goodness of people. Sometimes we'd argue with him. We'd say, 'The basic goodness of *some* people, Papa.' But he'd shake his head and say, 'It's there, God put it there in all of us. But sometimes—in some of us—it never has a chance to bloom, not even to sprout a little.'"

After the Soderbergs left *Guiding Light* to write *As the World Turns*, the show went through three other headwriters—James Gentile, Robert Cenedella and again James Lipton—that made ten different writing regimes in just as many years! What was obviously needed were writers who would bring continuity to *Guiding Light* and bring the show "into the twentieth century." In 1975, Procter & Gamble found them in Bridget and Jerome Dobson, who successfully contemporized *Guiding Light* over the next five years.

In 1972, Guiding Light celebrated its thirty-fifth year on the air and twentieth on television. Joining in the festivities from left to right: executive producer Lucy Rittenberg, wardrobe mistress Flossie Richard, Theo Goetz, Charita Bauer, and Ellen Demming. Flossie was a legend around the set, having begun her show business career performing on the Mississippi River boats in 1910.

At the same party: creator Irna Phillips, former producer-writer David Lesan, and headwriters Edith Sommer and Robert Soderberg.

"When we were writing *General Hospital*," Bridget Dobson recalled, "it was a reflection of my parents. [Bridget's parents were Frank and Doris Hursley, the creators of *General Hospital*.] So, *Guiding Light* was our first time out of the nest. It was a terribly exciting period. We experimented and it was a growth period for us. Also, we got out away from all the fluff that used to be on, like when you began a scene, the doorbell rang, a person answered the door, asked whether he could take your coat, asked how you were, etcetera. We quickly cut that fluff and got right into the dramatic conflict.

"There was no sexuality on the show. Some of the people seemed homely and badly dressed. Too many of the men sounded like each other, and the characters weren't distinctive in the way they talked or acted. There was no humor, no sass. I like sass! But the family structure was very good and we built upon that. When you have such good actors like Charita, Don, and Mart it wasn't difficult to keep the Bauers in focus. We brought in the Stapleton sisters, Ed was paired with Rita, and Eve went with Ben—that was our young love story. Then we brought in the Spaulding and Marler families. [On November 7, 1977 the show expanded to an hour, thus necessitating a flood of new characters.] But we thought of the Bauer family as central and we interwove the new families with the Bauers. The new characters were almost always involved in one way or another with the Bauer family."

The Dobsons wrote beautifully constructed stories, centering on a series of intricate romantic triangles—Ed, Rita, Holly—and even quadrangles—Jackie and Justin Marler and Elizabeth and Alan Spaulding. They also brought sexual themes and regular injections of eroticism to the show. Times had certainly changed since the early sixties when producer Lucy Rittenberg was called on the carpet for allowing a scene to fade out on Mike Bauer leaning over Julie Conrad's bed. "The sponsors and network were shocked and upset at the intimation that Mike and Julie were about to make love," Lucy recalled. "We were told never to let anything like that ever happen again. Of course, nowadays anything goes—and usually does!"

The Dobsons zeroed in on Roger Thorpe (played by Michael Zaslow), who was to become the sexiest villain the soaps had ever known. Roger seduced both of Ed Bauer's wives and Ed's half sister as well. "Well that does seem a bit perverse," Bridget laughingly admitted. "But there is a slight bit of perversity in us. That's me. That's my husband. We're ambivalent people. We always strive for purity and always miss! Roger was our ambivalent villain, our catalyst, and he motivated story and character. The Rita-Roger-Ed story we loved writiing, and I'm very proud of the Holly-Roger marital rape storyline. We based that on the Rideout case and researched it at the Rape Crisis Center in Oregon, where Mrs. Rideout had gone.

"Thinking back on it, it was one of the happiest times in our writing career. We got along very well with the producer Allen Potter [who had taken over when Lucy Rittenberg left the show in 1976.] We found our voices as writers and behind the scenes we had a wonderful time." The Dobsons wrote *As the World Turns* for a while afterwards, then created *Santa Barbara*, which runs opposite *Guiding Light* and the show that started it all for the two, *General Hospital*. How does Bridget feel about competing with her parents' show and *Guiding Light*, for which she and her husband did some of their best work? "Well, I don't know," Bridget said mischievously, "If I had my druthers, *Santa Barbara* would be number one in the ratings, *General Hospital* number two, and I don't know where *Guiding Light* would be—maybe number three?"

Before location shooting was in vogue, romantic picnics took place inside a studio padded with fake grass and trees. Maureen Garrett and Mart Hulswit rehearse their roles as Holly and Ed, 1977. (Al Rosenberg/Sterling's Magazines.)

You'd need a drink, too. Stephen Yates (who played Ben McFarren) and Janet Grey (Eve) in a morning rehearsal, 1978. (Al Rosenberg/Sterling's Magazines.)

After the Dobsons left in January 1980, *Guiding Light* entered into an even more critically and commercially spectacular period. Everybody was talking about what writer Douglas Marland and producer Gloria Monty had done with *General Hospital*, bringing the show from the bottom of the ratings barrel to number three in a little more than a year. When Douglas left *General Hospital*—Gloria wanted him to move to California where the production was based, and he declined—the writer was nabbed by Procter & Gamble, and Douglas wrote the ailing *As the World Turns* for thirteen weeks before becoming headwriter of *Guiding Light*.

"What I loved about *Guiding Light*," Douglas recalled at the *As the World Turns* studio, where he once again serves as headwriter, "was its rich history, strong roots, and its wonderful family structure. But watching the show, I was struck by two things. Everyone in Springfield was over twenty-five years old—even the "young" characters, Ben and Eve and Hope—and there were no teenagers. Also, I felt all the characters—the Spauldings, Marlers, and Bauers—led a comfortable lifestyle. There were no 'have-nots' on the show. Thus the creation of the Reardon family. And I attached my new characters with the core characters—Kelly was Ed's godson, Mike was involved with Morgan's mother, Roger Thorpe was hiding out at the Reardon's boarding house.

"Another dilemma was that I was told I had three months to get rid of Roger Thorpe," Douglas remembered. After nine years of maliciousness, the character was unredeemable, and actor Michael Zaslow wanted to move on to other work. (Zaslow later returned to daytime on *One Life to Live* as David Renaldi.) "But that was a wonderful plum to be handed as a writer," Douglas continued, "to devise a demise for as famous a character as Roger was. It couldn't be a *small* death—like a knifing or a shooting—it had to be spectacular."

And so it was. Taped on location in the Dominican Republic, Roger fell to his death off the side of a cliff, his hand slipping out of Ed Bauer's. This put an end to the sensational performance of Michael Zaslow, who began on the show April 1, 1971 and left exactly nine years later on April Fools' Day, 1980. Viewers never got to see the body; it was decided that to show the battered corpse would be too grotesque. Still, the audience hoped that Roger, who seemed to have more lives than a cat, would pop up in the future.

When the 1979–80 Emmy Awards rolled around, *Guiding Light* submitted a tape which contained scenes from three different shows: Holly shooting Roger, Roger remembering his rapes of Holly and Rita, and Roger chasing a pregnant Rita through a carnival hall of mirrors to a recording of the Barbra Streisand-Donna Summer duet *Enough is Enough*. Although Michael Zaslow obviously gave the finest performance by an actor that year, he failed to be nominated. However, *Guiding Light* was recognized as Outstanding Daytime Drama Series. This was to be the beginning of *Guiding Light*'s Emmy sweep. Douglas Marland's writing team won for the next two seasons, and the show took the top award again for the 1981–82 season.

Guiding Light continued to keep its older audience, but with the explosion of youth in Springfield, younger viewers started flocking to the show, and the ratings soared. But the famous Kelly-Morgan-Nola story triangle almost did not come off as planned. "I took a lot of time and care with these characters," Douglas recalled. "They were to be my young love story. I remembered asking my niece, who was fifteen at the time, what would be your biggest fantasy? And she said, 'If a college guy thought I was the most special thing in the world.' Not one of her high-school peers—not a Tim Werner but a Kelly Nelson.

"So when I got into it, I wanted to get beyond the fantasy and tell a very moral story: what happens to a seventeen-year-old who has sexual relations but is not emotionally prepared to deal with it. In my long-term story projection Morgan was going to have to deal with her confusion and an entire sequence of other problems. But the following summer, Kelly and Morgan would be married. Well, CBS Program Practices called me the morning of the taping of the seduction scene and said, 'no go.' Well, I said, there goes a whole year of story down the drain! And they countered with, 'Aren't you telling America that a seventeen-year-old who has sex this summer will be rewarded next summer with marriage?'

"I pointed out that no one watching could possibly know that Kelly and Morgan would, indeed, be married the next year. The two were going to have a horrendous year in between. I'm telling a moral story and you're making it less so. Finally, I drew a bead on what was really going on: that Kelly—the

The Laurel Falls Gang, 1980. From top left: Marsha Clark (who played Hillary Bauer), John Wesley Shipp (Dr. Kelly Nelson), Tom Nielsen (Floyd Parker), Denise Pence (Katie Parker), Lisa Brown (Nola Reardon), and Kevin Bacon (Tim Werner). Kevin Bacon became a major film personality after leaving Guiding Light, *starring in* Footloose *and* Diner.

man—would walk away scot-free but the girl has to really suffer. They wanted Morgan to be saddled with a pregnancy! I said that I didn't want to touch that tired story—it had been done to death. This is a story about a girl who loses her virginity and is not equipped emotionally to cope with a sexual relationship. I wanted to tell kids out there: think very hard before you take this step because it's a much bigger step than you think it is. It's more than a physical encounter—it's what happens afterwards that's important.

"So, out of sheer frustration, I said that I was going to call up Gloria Steinem and every feminist group I could think of and tell them that CBS says

Among headwriter Douglas Marland's many innovations was the introduction of musical talents who performed on the show. Clockwise: Ashford & Simpson, Tom Nielsen and Pretty Boy Floyd, Judy Collins, and Maurice Gibb of the Bee Gees.

it's fine for a young man to have sex, but it's not all right for a young woman because she has to pay—she has to get pregnant. Finally, CBS gave in."

Kelly, Morgan, and Nola were expertly cast with John Wesley Shipp, Kristen Vigard, and Lisa Brown, respectively, in the parts. "When we were casting Morgans," Douglas laughed, "Betty Rea—who is the best casting director in the business—sent me a tape of seven Morgans, and there was an extraordinary creature on the tape who was nowhere close to the concept of Morgan. She was Lisa Brown. I kept watching this test because I was fascinated by this actress with this marvelous reedy voice, and I wondered why in the world Betty had included her on the tape. Betty said, 'I know she's wrong for Morgan, but some show is going to grab this girl, Douglas, so I suggest you grab her first.' So Lisa was cast as Nola, who was introduced a couple months earlier than planned, and it turned out to be wonderful comic relief with Nola snooping around Roger Thorpe at the boarding house."

The mail poured in to CBS during this period. John Shipp consistently received more letters than any other performer on the show (with more than one letter requesting a photo of the muscular John in a pair of Speedos). However, Lisa Brown's mail was quite different. So energetic and convincing was Lisa's performance as the nasty Nola that the actress, according to a CBS official, began receiving the most intense hate mail of any daytime performer since *As the World Turns*'s Eileen Fulton two decades before. The story brewed for over a year and on July 27, 1981 it exploded in a very special *Guiding Light* episode.

Usually the show opened with three or four short scenes to establish the characters and action that would take place in that episode. But not that day. The world seemed to stop as Kelly finally confronted Nola and exposed her as a fraud and a liar. The show opened with a ten-minute scene between Kelly and Nola, then there was a commercial break. When the show continued there was another ten-minute scene between Kelly and Nola—in all, a twenty-minute *tour de force* of acting, directing, and writing. "I felt the audience deserved this payoff," Douglas said. "They deserved the catharsis of Nola getting her comeuppance. Nola had been so devious, so rotten—and she had been a hair away from ruining two people's lives. And when she got home, her mother and brother gave it to her. It was a day of reckoning for Nola.

"What was interesting about this show was that it was the first episode to be taped after the writer's strike was settled. It was so important because we had been working up to this confrontation for over a year. So, as the actors were on the set, I was literally phoning in the dialogue from Connecticut. The

Nola's cinematic fantasies were some of the most memorable sequences in daytime drama history. Michael Tylo and Lisa Brown play a variation of Now, Voyager.

director, Harry Eggart, told John Shipp and Lisa Brown to just play it and don't worry about the cameras because they would be covered. I think why the scenes were so effective because they were so spontaneous, off-the-cuff. It was exciting and got everyone's juices flowing; it was a team effort that really boosted the backstage morale.

"After Nola's comeuppance, she had to change, so I came up with an idea that would move her into a new realm of audience identification. Nola always related to everything on the basis of old movies—she used to make Kelly laugh with her obsession. The Reardons couldn't afford to see the current films, so their TV lounge is where Nola took in every old movie and created a fantasy life for herself. She was always talking about *A Place in the Sun* with Elizabeth Taylor and Montgomery Clift. So when Nola was on the bus to get her abortion—

which she decided against later—I thought this would be a terrific place to let her see herself as Elizabeth Taylor—to let her imagination flow. That worked so well that we did other movie takeoffs."

These cinematic fantasies were sensational and Lisa Brown was a revelation in them. The show did variations of *Now Voyager, Dark Victory, Casablanca, Wuthering Heights*, and *Shipmates Forever*. (The latter was all singing and all dancing.) The audience loved it and Leslie Fiedler, probably the country's finest literary critic, raved about Marland's writing and called the fantasies "a breakthrough in television." And Bette Davis herself wrote the show a lovely fan letter, which ended with the postscript, "Tell Nola she has it!"

"I guess my favorite fantasies were of the Bette Davis films," Douglas admitted when asked what he thought were the highlights of his tenure with the

Play it again, Sam: Guiding Light's *take-off on* Casablanca *with Michael Tylo, Lisa Brown, and John Wesley Shipp.*

An all-singing, all-dancing Shipmates Forever *fantasy with Lisa showing off her musical comedy talents. Lisa was starring on Broadway in* 42nd Street *at the same time as her* Guiding Light *role.*

Guiding Light's version of
The Wizard of Oz with Lisa
as Dorothy/Nola, Michael
Tylo as the Scarecrow,
Gregory Beecroft as the Tin
Man, and William
"Courage" Roerick as the
Cowardly Lion.

Headwriter Douglas Marland nabbed two Emmy Awards for his work on Guiding Light.

show. "Let me see. Vanessa was also hilarious. Remember, she was the first female flasher on television! And only Maeve Kinkead could have carried it off with such class. On a more serious note, Jennifer on trial—in those final scenes the acting and directing were superb. The unravelling of the Carrie story when she came in exhausted and confessed everything to Ross; I thought Jane Elliot was terribly moving."

Douglas Marland left the show after disagreements with producer Allen Potter, who felt the ratings during the height of the Carrie story were not sufficient to carry on with with future storylines for Carrie. Subsequently, actress Jane Elliot was dropped from the show, and Douglas filled out the remaining months on his contract and quit. "I had a deep emotional commitment to the show," Douglas said. "The ratings were very healthy, but the producer and I didn't see eye to eye on very much. I had a six-month story projection for Carrie and I thought it was a terrible cheat to the audience not to see Carrie's multipersonality problems resolved, to see her become a real, whole person.

"I loved *Guiding Light*. It has been successful for fifty years because it stayed so close to its core—family, strong values of honesty and loyalty. The show has a heritage. The secret of being a headwriter on a long-running show is to keep your balance, don't swing too heavily toward one genre of storytelling or all new characters. Love the core or don't write for the show. Respect the audience that has been listening, watching for years."

After Douglas's departure, the show seemed to collapse. Pat Falken Smith took over for a couple months as writer and tried to untangle the complex mystery of Quint-Mark-Mona, but the story became even more convoluted. Falken Smith's stint with the show was also marked by a bizarre plot turn in which a house that was being moved crashed into the Reardon's boarding house, thus creating room for Tony's bar, Company. L. Virginia Browne's brief tenure as headwriter was highlighted by the introduction of Grant Aleksander, the most exciting young actor in daytime in years, as Phillip Spaulding. Browne also pushed Phillip and Ed Bauer's son Rick (who was no longer being called Freddy—thank God) to the forefront of the drama.

Guiding Light was in a slump and it took the efforts of the *Texas* team of producer Gail Kobe and writers Richard Culliton and Pamela Long Hammer for the show to come back with a vengeance. Behind the scenes, Gail worked feverishly to give the show a new look. She set out to improve the sets, the lighting, the costumes, the music, and the directing. As one admiring stagehand said recently, "It was pretty status quo around here until Gail Kobe started kicking ass. We have a country club set that looks like a real country club. Rick's apartment looks like somebody really lives there. And Alex's library is a beaut. You know, she threw out the teleprompters. Those actors have to really cut the mustard now."

Richard and Pam finished off the inherited, byzantinelike storylines with a flourish, and transformed *Guiding Light* back into a family show, constructing stories around the Bauers, Spauldings, Reardons, Chamberlains, and especially the Lewises. They also introduced perhaps the most appealing young-love stories ever on daytime. Remember Beth falling in love with the self-destructive, alienated Phillip at the senior prom? Or Beth and Phillip hiding out in New York from Bradley Raines? Or when Mindy hilariously seduced Rick locked in a hospital linen closet? These teenage characters were offbeat and lovable, and the audience began to respond.

The older characters received equal time—remember Vanessa and Nola wearing the same Scarlett O'Hara dress at the antebellum ball?—and the show reaffirmed its across-the-board appeal. In the first half of 1984, the new *Guiding Light* had added two million viewers to its audience while the competition, the seemingly invincible *General Hospital*, lost five million as a result of Luke and Laura's departure. *Guiding Light* zoomed to the number one spot in the ratings for three weeks straight. And the introduction of Beverlee McKinsey, hands down the most sophisticated presence ever to grace daytime drama, as Alexandra Spaulding brought new critical and commercial interest to the show.

But trouble loomed ahead: in October 1984, the Bauer family—the focus of the show for almost four decades—was dealt a series of devastating blows. Hillary Bauer was suddenly killed off, her brother Mike was written out of the show, and the actor playing Ed Bauer was replaced. Hope Bauer had been written out months before and many of the wonderful characters Douglas Marland had created were being phased out.

"In retrospect," executive producer Gail Kobe explained, "it was a mistake. The Bauers meant a great deal to the audience and it was unfortunate that these changes took place within a few weeks of each other. But, of course,

Remember when Nola, played by Lisa Brown, and Vanessa, played by Maeve Kinkead, showed up at a Civil War–theme ball in the same Scarlett-at-the-barbeque gown? The fur flew.

"Say the secret woid": Judi Evans, Grant Aleksander, Krista Tesreau, and Michael O'Leary display an unusual reverence for their craft.

Charita was ill and we had no control over that. The recasting of Ed was necessary because Peter Simon wanted to move on to other projects. As for Mike, Hillary, and Hope, the writers, performers, and management disagreed on the development of the characters. It was decided for a variety of reasons that the characters be written out. Of course, we received a lot of negative mail about the changes. So, don't be surprised when Mike and Hope are written back into the story in the future."

Pam and her new co-headwriter Jeff Ryder soon zeroed in on the Lewis and Shayne families, Beth and Lujack's romance, and a slew of adventure stories. Two years before, Charles Jay Hammer served briefly as associate writer, before joining the cast as smart-talking, roving reporter Fletcher Reade. Jay met Pam when they both were acting on *Texas*. They were married, Pam was handed the headwriting position of *Texas* and the show became a cult hit over the next six months. When that show was cancelled—it received the most

In this 1984 publicity shot, Grant Aleksander presented Judi Evans with a very special valentine.

protest mail NBC had ever received for a daytime *or* prime-time show—Pam became headwriter of *Guiding Light* for almost three years. She then took a leave of absence from the show to have another child and decided not to return. A few months after her departure, Pam and her writing team nabbed an Emmy for Outstanding Writing.

"Bradley Raines was Pam's favorite character creation," Jay said, recalling Pam's three years with the show. "He exemplified evil and he forced good people to react in various ways. Some behaved better under the pressures, others cracked under Bradley's evil, some overcame their fears—he was a great catalyst for drama. Of course, there was a reason why he was the way he was and Pam explored that. There is a dark side in many of Pam's characters. The thing

Nurse Lillian! Bea Reardon!
Get ahold of yourselves.
Tina Sloan and Lee Lawson
check out the assets of
visiting Chippendale star
Scott Marlowe.

```
                Recently Overheard in Springfield:

    Alex:              Nothing holds a marriage together
                       more than mutual avarice.
    Phillip:           What about love?
    Alex:              I'll buy you some.

    Alex to India:     Are you leaving? I hope it's
                       something I've said.

    India:             What we had was a fluke, a one time
                       affair . . .
    Simon:             Darling, you can't count.

    Lujack to Beth:    Don't be afraid, babe . . .
                       Remember—shadows only mean there's
                       light somewhere.

    Warren to India:   A word to the wily . . .

    Jackson:           I'm an artiste.
    Alex:              Says who? The clerk who sold you that
                       earring?
```

that makes Fletcher interesting is not the obvious—his cute buns, his dimples, his sense of humor—but that Fletcher has a story—a secret—that he had a three-year-old daughter whose guts were blown out in front of him and Fletcher has a tremendous amount of guilt about it. He has his dark side; he keeps a cover on the part of his life that he can't bring himself to show. But the audience knows he's tap-dancing.

"The character Pam created that [the actress Pam] would most like to play is Reva. Pam loves Reva's warmth, her impulsiveness. No, Reva is not really similar to Reena on *Texas*. Pam developed the character, but it was created by the Corringtons. Reena was impulsive but she was privileged, spoiled. Reva is free-spirited and she came from very humble roots. Audiences were drawn to Reena's outrageousness, but audiences are drawn to Reva's humanity. It's Reva's humanity that makes her special."

```
H.B. to Reva:       You and temptation were made for
                    each other.

Lt. Saunders to Nurse Lillian:    Lillian, I've
                    arrested practically your entire
                    family. Isn't it time you started
                    calling me Jeff?

Sally to Hawk:      Me? I haven't felt guilty about
                    anything since I started wearing
                    lipstick.

Alex to Lujack:     Let me take you shopping. I've been
                    known to give ''charge'' new
                    meaning.

Calla on the phone with Jackie O (in a fantasy):    I
                    know you want the rights to my
                    autobiography, but I'm so busy these
                    days, the only free day I have is
                    next Friday . . . Caroline's wedding
                    shower? Well, which is more
                    important to you? . . . Fine. See you
                    next Friday.
```

In the 1984–85 season *Guiding Light* was nominated for Outstanding Daytime Drama Series, Outstanding Writing (Pam and Jeff and their writing team), while Michael O'Leary (Rick Bauer) and Maeve Kinkead (Vanessa Chamberlain Lewis) were nominated as Outstanding Juvenile/Young Man and Outstanding Supporting Actress. The show won awards for Outstanding Directing while Larry Gates (H.B. Lewis) and the radiant Kim Zimmer (Reva Shayne Lewis took awards as Outstanding Supporting Actor and Outstanding Actress. Charita Bauer was honored posthumously with a Lifetime Achievement Award, which her son, Michael Crawford, accepted on her behalf.

"It was a difficult situation all around," Gail Kobe said, recalling the time Charita fell ill and had to have her leg amputated. "We told her if she could work, we would certainly provide her with work and make every effort to make it comfortable for her on the set. I suggested the prosthesis story to her because I knew she had something to contribute and I wanted her to know she was needed here. I think we did the story very responsibly. You can't do a story

In the 1984–85 season Vincent Irizarry became a fan favorite as the pugnacious Lujack. (Al Rosenberg/Sterling's Magazines.)

The cast of the Fall of 1985. Top row, left to right: Eric Brooks (as Dr. Louie Darnell), Alice Oakes (Nurse Jodie), Michael Wilding (Jackson Freemont), John Martinuzzi (David Preston), Frances Fisher (Suzette Saxon), Charles Jay Hammer (Fletcher Reade), Susan Pratt (Dr. Claire Ramsey), Richard Van Vleet (Dr. Ed Bauer), Ellen Dolan (Maureen Bauer), sleepy Lee Lawson (Bea Reardon), Jaison Walker (I.Q.), and David Little (Lt. Jeff Saunders). Middle row: Jordan Clarke (Billy Lewis), Christian Davies (H.B. Lewis III), William Roerick (Henry Chamberlain), Krista Tesreau (Mindy Lewis), Mark Lewis (Kurt Corday), Kristi Ferrell (Roxie Shayne), Judi Evans (Beth Raines), Vincent Irizarry (Lujack), Tina Sloan (Lillian Raines), and Warren Burton (Warren Andrews). Bottom row: Mary Kay Adams (India Spaulding), John Bolger (Phillip Spaulding), Beverlee McKinsey (Alexandra Spaulding), Leslie Denniston (Maeve Sampson), Larkin Malloy (Kyle Sampson), Kim Zimmer (Reva Shayne), Larry Gates (H.B. Lewis), Patricia Barry (Miss Sally Gleason), and Gil Rogers (Hawk Shayne).

like that or Beth's abuse storyline or Reva's attempted suicide without doing it responsibly, with care and with truth. The scene in which Bert dropped a cup and couldn't bend over and pick up the pieces really got to me. It was clear Bert did not burst into tears out of self-pity, but out of sheer frustration. It was a story of courage.

"We had dealt with Charita's illness as Bert, so when Charita died none of us could cope with it. We thought it was important to keep the character alive—it was important that Rick could pick up the phone and say, 'Grandma, I need you.' We had a generation growing up with her, looking up to her, so it wasn't fair to dramatize Bert's illness and then just cavalierly kill her off. But it didn't work because we would look at scripts with telephone calls and letters from Bert and it was so depressing for us who knew and loved Charita. And it was confusing for the audience: they knew Charita had died, so why wasn't Bert dead too? So we waited exactly a year after Charita's death to deal with Bert's death. And we celebrated Bert and Charita with a service and montage of pictures of her on the show through the past thirty-five years."

It was an end of an era for *Guiding Light*, and the beginning of another. And there's good news for the future: new executive producer Joe Willmore and headwriter Sheri Anderson plan to bring back favorite performers, reestablish the Bauer family as the focus of the show, and revitalize Springfield with the youthful offspring of the Reardons and Spauldings. After three thousand episodes on radio and ten thousand episodes on TV, the show roars ahead.

When *Guiding Light* was transferred to television, it replaced a serial called *The First Hundred Years*, which fell short of its goal by ninety-eight and a half years. *Guiding Light* has already broken all the records in broadcasting history by celebrating its fiftieth anniversary on the air. Is there any doubt that the indestructible *Guiding Light* will reach the century mark? Imagine Papa Rick Bauer regalling his great-grandchildren with memories of Bert—not to mention his impressions of Jimmy Carter or his embarrassed grin when someone mentions that the hospital grapevine gossip of the day was "stud" Rick's conquest of the hot-to-trot Dr. Claire Ramsey. It's enough to make you want to stick around this crazy world for *Guiding Light*'s Centennial Celebration!

A Tribute to Charita Bauer *2*

Before her death in 1985, Charita Bauer had the distinction of playing a single character the longest in broadcasting history. Charita joined *Guiding Light* as Bert Bauer (is there anyone who doesn't know that the last names were a coincidence?) in February 1950 and continued to play the part until December 10, 1984. She began her career as a child model for Macy's, but when the store asked her to model long underwear, Charita refused and was let go. At age nine she made her debut on Broadway in Christopher Morley's *Thunder on the Left*. She was the original Little Mary in Clare Boothe Luce's acclaimed, all-female comedy *The Women*, which ran for two years on Broadway with Charita playing every performance.

Charita began to work regularly in children's radio shows, including the prize-winning fantasy series *Let's Pretend*, playing such diverse parts as a Chinese boy, a mosquito, and a blind hillbilly. After graduating from the Professional Children's School, Charita did more theatre work and her career in radio soap operas flourished. She played Lanette in *Our Gal Sunday*, Gail Carver in *Lora Lawton*, Maude Mason in *Maude's Diary*, Susan Wakefield in *The Right to Happiness*, Fran Cummings in *Second Husband*, and Millie Baxter in *Young Widder Brown*.

Before joining the radio cast of *Guiding Light*, Charita was part of the prime-time TV explosion of the late forties. She was a regular on *The Aldrich Family* as Mary Aldrich in the 1949–50 season and had a running role on *Mama*

Charita as a child model.

Charita (right) as Little Mary opposite Betty Lawford in the Broadway production The Women.

As a radio personality in the forties.

With son Michael, 1947.

(also called *I Remember Mama*) as Gwendolyn Carter, Katrin's best friend. (Since *Mama* was broadcast live and rarely put on film, there are few episodes that survive. But two episodes featuring Charita are available for viewing at the Museum of Broadcasting in New York.)

But of course, Charita will be always remembered as Bert. When *Guiding Light* came around, Charita's career was very hot; she had been unemployed for only two weeks since she was a child. She asked her father if she was limiting her career by signing with the show. He said, "Try it, it's only for two years." Well, two years stretched into thirty-five. A pivotal heroine in the fifties and sixties ("When Agnes Nixon wrote the show, I did my best work," she declared), Bert became a supporting player in the seventies and eighties, the symbol of hope and reassurance to the Bauers and their friends.

Wherever she went, Charita was recognized: stepping out of a gondola in Venice, walking into the Savoy Hotel in London, or backstage at the Met meeting Grace Bumbry. Always, it was the same reaction, "Why Bert Bauer, what are you doing here?" Even the Manhattan hookers heading home at dawn would stop Charita walking her dog Shakespeare and fuss over both of them. Charita never grew tired of meeting fans and tried valiantly to keep up with her mail. A typical letter to Charita, this one dated January 26, 1977, read: "My 78-year-old mom has faithfully followed *The Guiding Light* since it first began and it

On I Remember Mama *as
Gwendolyn Carter opposite
Rosemary Rice as Katrin.*

Charita, you're on Guiding Light, *not on* As the World Turns, *remember? That's Glenn Walken (left) who played her onscreen son, Michael Bauer, and Michael Crawford, her off-screen son, 1956.*

is one of her greatest pleasures! I too have watched the past few years and feel as if you are part of our lives, seeing you each day. We laugh and cry and *feel* each experience! Many times I have mentioned how much I'd love to have a friend like Bert Bauer."

In the 1977–78 season, Bert had her first major storyline in years as her troublesome, alcoholic husband reappeared after an absence of almost ten years. It was sheer melodrama, but Charita's performance as Bert going from shock to anger to forgiveness was one of the season's highlights. The next year the actress was presented with the Outstanding Mother Award by the National Mother's Day Committee for heading up two families, each with a son named Michael. (Her offscreen son, Michael Crawford, was born in 1946; her soap son was born in 1952, when the show was on radio.) In 1983, she and a handful of other *Guiding Light* regulars appeared in the prime-time TV movie *The Cradle Will Rock*.

That same year, after she finished up a superb storyline in which Bert befriended a dying man, Charita was awarded an Emmy for Lifetime Achieve-

ment. (In 1985, she was posthumously honored with an Emmy for Distinguished Service to Daytime Television.) In the fall of 1983, Charita started having pain in her leg. It turned out to be a circulatory problem, and when other medical procedures failed, she had to have her leg amputated. She spent five months recovering and getting adjusted to her artificial limb, then returned to the show and re-created her real life story in the hope that it would be helpful to other disabled people and their families.

"At first Charita resisted the prosthesis story," executive producer Gail Kobe recalled, "she thought the audience wouldn't like it at all. We disagreed, of course, and when Charita told me that she did not want to be paid for the time she was off work, I told her to stop being so proud and loud, and we had to laugh. That broke the ice, and Charita saw that she had something to con-

With Don Stewart, who played the grown-up Mike Bauer, 1977.

tribute. As it turned out, the audience loved the story—they were so happy to see her back."

Charita remained on the show for six months, but left when again she fell ill. "People never realized how ill my mother really was," Charita's son Michael explained. "She was the type of person who would bull right through the worst of times. My mother was a very private person, yet she was also the consummate politician. She never rubbed management the wrong way; she was a team player. She had a great deal of appreciation that she was working. She never took her role on *Guiding Light* for granted. Every time her contract was renewed, she was slightly surprised."

Charita died February 28, 1985. A few days later, actor Jerry verDorn made the announcement to viewers with the words, "The continuing story

Guiding Light is dedicated to the memory of Charita Bauer, whose portrayal of Bert Bauer has illuminated our lives for over thirty-five years. The spirit of Charita Bauer, her strength and her courage, her grand good humor, her passion for life, and her humanity have touched us all. She has graced our lives at *Guiding Light* and will be with us always."

"Jerry's announcement said it all, so succinctly and lovingly," Ellen Demming, one of Charita's closest friends, recalled. "The word 'generosity' was not used, but implied. Generosity was a natural, unthinking impulsiveness on Charita's part. She began her march of gifts to us when we bought our first house—lovely things, from Waterford crystal to sterling silver. I remember we were in W. & J. Sloane's one day, and I stopped to admire a set of pitchers. Three days later, they arrived at my home!"

The mere mention of Charita's name today brings broad grins from the members of the backstage crew. "Aw, that Charita she was a great gal," said one. "She didn't have a phony bone in her body." Said another: "She was like everybody's mother, she knew everybody by name, and she always had a kind word for all." One crew member remembered that he had asked Charita to participate in a 4-H Club fair, and she left a White House dinner to fulfill her promise. "Yes," Locke Wallace, the stage manager, concurred, "Charita was a great lady, but I have always thought of Charita as an artist first and foremost—an actress who really cared. I would see her on stage in other projects, and I saw the *joie de vivre* she brought to the roles. She had a rare gift: watching her even in the most simple of scenes, she made you feel happy."

On The Set *3*

You arrive with apprehension at the CBS studios in lower Manhattan, expecting to be ushered immediately into the wonderful world of Springfield. Will you be welcomed by Reva Shayne's twinkling smile or India Spaulding's wisecracks? Instead, you are greeted with a dark, old warehouse with dozens of workers milling about, barking orders, and trading quips—more like *Hill Street Blues* than *Guiding Light*.

Sitting next to you in the waiting area is a sleek young beauty using yellow magic marker to highlight the audition scene she's probably memorized 22,000 times. A ten-year-old boy sits across, also studying a script, with not a care in the world. His mother gets up, brushes his hair, and sits down. A minute later, mama gets up again, brushes his hair, and sits down. Betty Rea, the casting director, comes out and asks the boy, "Do you need any more time?" The boy spells his answer: 'n, o.' Betty is amused but not undaunted, and the little darlin' follows her down the hall.

Then the actors start filing down the hall. Why, there's Melinda Sue Lewis Spaulding Corday—such a little person for such a long name. My God, she even remembers you, even though it has been over a year and a half since you were introduced. Make a note: Mindy, and her alter-ego Krista Tesreau, are gonna come off good in this book. There's John Bolger, who plays Phillip, looking dapper in his F. Scott Fitzgerald duds. How tall is he anyway? Beverlee McKinsey smiles totally unlike her character, the snobby Alexandra Spaulding.

Don't say that she's your favorite actress—she'll think you a boob. Mention *Texas*, instead. "Oh, I loved that show," says Beverlee, "it was like a real family. We have the same feeling here, too." Then she's off to her dressing room, or drawing room, or wherever ex-baronesses go to get wicked.

It is nine o'clock in the morning, but the actors have already been there since before seven, going over their lines in the basement rehearsal hall. There the performers rehearse their dialogue with the director, with special emphasis on the line readings and the meaning of the scenes. Some dialogue the actors are uncomfortable with is tossed out or changed. On the set the action is blocked: where the actors move, what camera follows their movements and when. Once this "dry" rehearsal is completed, the director joins the producer in the control booth for a dress rehearsal. The scene begins with the director snapping instructions to the cameraman via earphones and waving his arms dramatically like Zubin Mehta leading the New York Philharmonic.

How times have changed: Charita in the first Bauer living room on TV, 1952.

Afterwards, the director and producer confer with a production assistant taking notes. The producer points out missed lines, inconsistencies, improvisations that she likes and doesn't like. "I want Maeve to be stronger in this scene," Hope Harmel Smith says. "India's messing up her entire life. Maeve should be in there knocking some sense into her." This acting note is delivered to actress Leslie Denniston, who agrees. "That improv by the newspaper editor is tasteless, it will have to go." Others in the control room groan. They like the improvisation, but Hope waves them aside. When someone points out that Jay Hammer, who plays ace reporter Fletcher Reade, rarely follows the words of the script, the producer and director agree that, given the nature of his character, the actor should be given some leeway. He gives the newspaper office scene spontaneity, a devil-may-care quality.

After the kinks are ironed out and the scene has been timed, it's ready to be taped. The actors' juices are flowing; they're "up"—sometimes too "up."

Alexandra Spaulding's library, 1986.

Before dress rehearsal, Larkin Malloy brushes up on his part as Kyle Sampson.

Mary Kay Adams, who plays the sophisticated India, momentarily forgets her line in the pressure and unleashes a string of unprintable comments. "That's French for, 'can we do it over again?'" Mary Kay asks. Everyone laughs and the tension is broken. Then the scene is started over again. This time it is done to everyone's satisfaction, and the next scene on the same set is blocked, dry and dress rehearsed and then taped. Afterwards, the actors move to a new set, and the process is started all over again.

Guiding Light is taped on a split schedule, the morning taping in the large downstairs studio, which contains five or six sets; the afternoon taping is in the smaller upstairs studio, which holds three or four sets. The morning session usually calls for a schedule of from 7 A.M. to 2 P.M.; the afternoon usually from 3 P.M. to 7 P.M. But that's on a good day. There can be endless delays, and when there are complicated scenes—party sequences, for example—the taping often ends at 11 P.M. There have been occasions when they didn't throw in the towel

*The control booth in which
the producer, director, and
assistants monitor what the
three cameras are taping
and select what will go into
the final "take."*

*While Leslie Denniston (who plays Maeve) and Larkin Malloy (Kyle) are
covered by one camera, Jay Hammer's (Fletcher) reaction will be caught
by the camera peeking out from the left.*

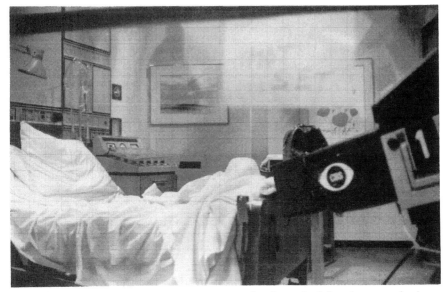

What's a hot set? It's when a set is not to be disturbed for the next day's taping (so everything will be in the same place as the day before); the technicians rope off the set.

An electrician adjusts the lights for an "outdoor" scene. Admiring his handiwork is actress-publicist Laurie Rovtar.

Lisby Larson (Calla), Beverlee McKinsey (Alex), and Rebecca Staab (Jesse)
rehearse a scene in which they argue over Simon.

until 4 o'clock in the morning! But the show has to produce an hour show a
day, five days a week, and no one leaves until the work is over.

But before the actors can even get out on the floor, the crew has to set
up. First the carpenters put up the sets, then the property department decorates
the set with furniture and knick-knacks, then the electricians light the set. To
break the monotony the crew joke and reminisce. One grip muses on the week-
long party scenes: "The only problem I have with these ongoing stories is that
in these parties some people are in the same damn dress for a week. Pee-yew!"
(Of course, nowadays there are duplicate outfits and overnight laundering.)
Then there was this actress a few years back who did her love scenes without
wearing any underwear, remembered another. "My God, was that set mobbed!"

One morning practically the entire downstairs studio is turned into the
"Club Zanzibar," the setting of Phillip's work-in-progress novel. Since the
scenes will be taped in black and white to capture the Roaring Twenties setting,
there are endless adjustments in makeup and costuming. There are dozens of

technicians making last-minute corrections—Beth's lipstick has to be lighter than India's, India's cigarette holder has to be found, and the smoke machine, billowing fog over the set to indicate cigarette smoke, can't overpower the actors. Since the set and costumes are so unusual for daytime drama, a still photographer is called in to record the effort for posterity. At her photo session with dozens of workers fussing over her, Mary Kay Adams vamps for the camera, declaring mischievously, "I love doing scenes alone."

Upstairs, Beverlee McKinsey and Shawn Thompson, who play Alex and Simon, prepare for a series of highly emotional scenes. A few weeks before, Beverlee's Alex had a series of scenes in which she finally accepted the death of her son, Brandon (Lujack). Beverlee, who doesn't stray a single word from the script, is exquisitely moving. After she finishes a beautifully written soliloquy, the control room roars with applause. Producer Hope Smith says, "That gave me chills!" Director Bruce Barry whistles. Today, both Beverlee and Shawn

After the rehearsal, a production assistant delivers acting notes to the actors from the producer in the control booth.

have emotionally explosive scenes, set in the Spaulding mausoleum, in which Simon cries out his frustration to the dead Lujack that he, Simon, will never be accepted as a Spaulding.

Shawn has only been on the show for a few months, but this is the first time he's been called upon to deliver emotional fireworks. Shawn paces nervously off the set, mouthing the dialogue to himself, getting himself psyched up for the "high" the scenes require. After lamenting at Lujack's grave, he must turn to face Alex in a no-holds-barred confrontation which has been brewing for weeks. Afterwards, there is a long monologue by Alex, remembering when Lujack was kidnapped from her two decades before, and then there is an overture of brotherly love by Simon and a reconciliation between the two.

During taping, Shawn, who is giving everything he's got, is too close to Lujack's crypt, and the camera loses him. Director Bruce Barry stops tape, apologizes, and Shawn understandably sighs in frustration. The scene is started

Lisby and Beverlee relax as the control booth checks the tape for any glitches.

March 24, 1986

Alex: I remember a time I was afraid I'd be alone
           for the rest of my life, too . . . I was just
           about your age. Eric and I were living with
           Brandon in Europe. We were so happy . . . I
           thought . . . Then—one morning—I woke up—
           and reached out to touch Eric—to hold him
           as I did every day before I got up. . . . Only
           he wasn't there. His side of the bed hadn't
           even been slept in. I sat up and looked
           around the room. It seemed so empty.
           Suddenly, I realized why. Eric's sheet
           music—reams of classical pieces—they were
           gone. All of them. At that moment—I knew
           for certain that Eric had left me. Pain
           washed over me . . . confusion . . . and
           then—panic. I rushed to the nursery—threw
           open the doors. The room was just as I had
           left it the night before—still with my dear
           child's sweet essence in the air. . . . But
           Brandon was gone . . . my baby was gone.

(ALEX WEEPS AT THE MEMORY. NOW SIMON REACHES OUT TO
HER. HOLDS HER. AFTER A BEAT:)

           I wanted to die that morning. But I wouldn't
           let myself. I forced myself to go on—for
           Brandon. I was determined to find him.

Simon: And you did . . .

Alex: Yes. . . . I did. . . . But for such a short
           time . . . I'd waited so long . . . and then
           . . . to lose him again. . . . I don't know if
           I'll ever recover from that . . . if I'll
           ever find the strength to reach out to
           someone else . . .

Simon: (TAKES A BEAT. THEN SOFTLY, SIMPLY:) I know. . . . I know. . . . But if you could only find that strength now . . . for both our sakes . . . I can love you, Alex. I can make sure you're never alone again. . . .

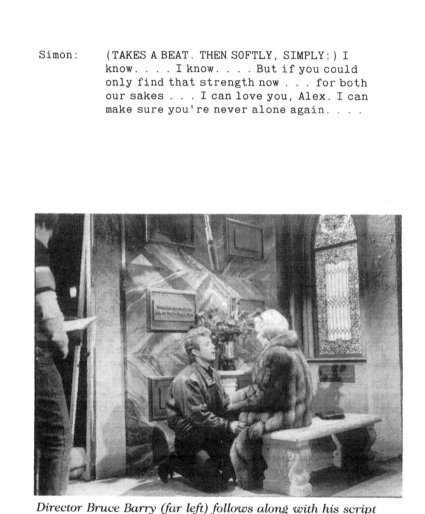

Director Bruce Barry (far left) follows along with his script as Shawn and Beverlee run through their lines before taping.

over again, but then there is a shadow from a microphone showing, and the action is halted once again. Shawn doesn't lose his temper; there is no time for temperament in fast-moving world of serial drama. Finally, the scene is finished, and the actor is spent.

Veteran Beverlee enters. Both actors have their lines down letter perfect, so there is minimal rehearsal. It is decided to just let the fireworks fly, and it is a wise decision because there is a rawness and vitality to the scene that well might have died with too much rehearsal. Then Beverlee recites her monologue with all the reverence and beauty the best actresses bring to a Tennessee Williams play. Alex and Simon are touchingly reunited, and Beverlee and Shawn walk off the set. Smiling.

Tomorrow, they start all over again.

The Story on Radio 4

Like so many others in the town of Five Points, Frances Holden saw the Reverend Doctor John Ruthledge as her last hope. Abandoning her eight-year-old son Ned to the minister's care, she vanished from the town and began a series of wanderings which stretched into the years.

When Frances was a sixteen-year-old, she had fallen hopelessly in love with the dashing Paul Holden, not realizing that Paul was a fortune hunter and only interested in her father's money. Their elopement caused an immediate strain between Frances and her father, and the young couple soon found themselves without funds. When Frances asked about Paul's business, Paul replied, "Frances, your naiveté is rather refreshing. I live, you might say, by my wits. I have a great aversion to working—an aversion which I don't think I shall ever overcome."

When Paul caught wind of Frances's pregnancy, he took a "job" in Philadelphia and made vague promises to send money. Three years later, Paul showed up at Frances's door and explained that he'd been sent to prison for selling fraudulent oil stocks. Over the next few years Paul made Frances's life hell, although she felt herself continually being drawn back to Paul, melting into his embraces and stupidly believing he would change.

Frances got a job as a cashier in a local store and Paul stole the key to the store, committed robbery, and subsequently Frances was implicated. Frances decided then to leave her son with Reverend Ruthledge and began a

Ed Prentiss as Ned Holden, Mercedes McCambridge as Mary Ruthledge, Peggy Fuller as Fredrika Lang, and Henrietta Tedro as the housekeeper, Ellen, 1937. Mercedes was going to college while acting on Guiding Light. *She shuttled back and forth on Chicago's El train from classes, to the* Guiding Light *microphones, to acting lessons, to night work on NBC radio—traveling, by her own estimation, 144 miles a day.* (Author's Collection.)

life on the run with her husband. She changed her name, but the law caught up with her and she spent time in prison.

Meanwhile, Ned grew up under the minister's care and fell in love with his daughter, Mary. Growing up with Ned, Mary considered Ned as a brother and fought romantic feelings, but finally gave in to her emotions and the two became engaged. Ned had become in the intervening years a well-respected writer, published a book, and with a hundred-dollar royalty check bought a brooch for Mary from Fredrika Lang, a charming woman he had met through Dr. Ruthledge. But a fine fraud Fredrika turned out to be: she had added an extra zero to his check and cashed it in for a thousand dollars!

Unknown to Ned, Fredrika was in fact Frances Holden, his mother. Paul had caught up with Fredrika and after threatening her, Fredrika gave Paul the check to get rid of him. Ned burst into Fredrika's home and accused her of raising the check. Of course, Paul had done it. At Fredrika's emotional ebb, Paul returned and told Fredrika that he was going to reveal himself as Ned's father. After all, Ned would not have either of his parents prosecuted. With that, Fredrika went berserk, pulled out a gun, and shot and killed Paul—anything to protect Ned.

Fredrika refused to offer any defense at her trial, even though Dr. Ruthledge guessed the truth and urged her to throw herself on the mercy of the court. She refused and was sentenced to die in the electric chair. But Dr. Ruthledge convinced the governor to give Fredrika a reprieve and the truth came out. Filled with hatred, Ned denounced his mother as a thief and a murderess, then ran away.

Mignon Schreiber as Mrs. Kransky, Raymond Edward Johnson as Ellis Smith, Ruth Bailey as Rose Kransky, and Willis Bouchey as Charles Cunningham, 1937. (Author's Collection.)

January 28, 1938

Paul: I said, my dear, that I think it's about
             time Ned knew who his parents were.

Fredrika: Paul, you don't know what you're saying.
             Are you suggesting that you came back
             here deliberately to tell Ned who we are?
             Are you low enough to want to ruin
             another life besides mine and your own?
             What has happened in the past concerns
             only you and me. What we've done, we've
             done to each other, but what you're
             contemplating now is too vile for words!
             You'd make him pay with his youth, his
             ambition and his happiness for your
             worthlessness. No, Paul, I won't permit
             that. We'll forget the check—we'll
             forget everything you've ever done in
             the past; but we'll go away from Five
             Points and we'll never come back. Ned is
             never to know who we are. Do you
             understand that? Never!

Paul: Never is a long time, Fredrika. As long
             as our son is doing so well, I can't see
             why he shouldn't want to help his
             parents.

Fredrika: Stop it! Do you hear me? Stop it! I can't
             stand it any longer. Liar, thief—I hate
             you. I hate you as I thought it wasn't
             possible to hate any human being.

Paul: Becoming hysterical, Fredrika, isn't
             going to help matters any. Surely you
             realize that.

```
Fredrika:      Paul, you and I are leaving Five Points.
               Now! Today!

Paul:          Speak for yourself, Fredrika. You may go
               if you like. I intend to stay. . . . Why
               are you opening that drawer?

Fredrika:      I have had this for some time. I've been
               saving it for just this purpose.

Paul:          A revolver? Put it away, Fredrika. As
               I've said on several occasions,
               dramatics don't become you. I've made up
               my mind to see Ned.

Fredrika:      (SHE SHOOTS HIM.) You'll never see Ned.
               (SHE SHOOTS HIM AGAIN.) No, Paul Holden,
               you'll never see Ned.
```

At loose ends, Ned became infatuated with Torchy Reynolds, a showgirl he met in San Francisco, and impulsively married her. When they returned to Five Points, Ned's fiancée Mary went into shock. But Mary realized that Torchy really cared for Ned and had brought about his emotional rehabilitation. Ultimately, however, Torchy came to the conclusion that Ned's heart belonged to Mary, and Torchy selflessly stepped aside. After Ned came to terms with himself and his mother, he and Mary were married.

Meanwhile, Dr. Ruthledge, who had won the affectionate nickname of "The Good Samaritan" over the years, settled union disputes and domestic quarrels and encouraged his flock through a series of powerful sermons to seek a fuller and more beautiful life for themselves and their families. These sermons touched on racial prejudice, man's need to help those less fortunate, and the futility of war.

Near Dr. Ruthledge and his church was a secondhand store owned by Abe Kransky, an Orthodox Jew, and his family. The Kranskys, who lived in tenement housing, had two children, Rose and Jacob. Rose was restless and hated her life in Five Points: "Poverty, gossipy neighbors, sordid surroundings, and no chance to get ahead." She liked and envied Mary Ruthledge, but in reality Mary was not that much better off. Yet Mary had the understanding father Rose did not, and Rose poured out her frustrations to the minister.

Rose wanted to go to night school to study shorthand and have a career as a secretary; her father wanted her to get married and raise a family. She felt that her old-fashioned parents would never adapt themselves to the ways of modern American life. Dr. Ruthledge told her that there was no reason for her not to pursue her dreams and he interceded for Rose. Dr. Ruthledge even lent her the money to begin her schooling.

Although her father kept pushing eligible young men at her, Rose found them all rough-edged and silly. When she finished her education, Rose went to work as a stenographer for Cunningham Publishing Company. One day, Charles Cunningham's secretary, Helen Ryder, attempted suicide. It was whispered in the office that Charles had thrown Helen over to marry a rich society woman. Rose stepped into Helen's job and her career took off.

Charles soon confided that his marriage to Celeste was not a happy one and Rose found herself falling in love with her boss. They had an affair and Charles promised Rose that he would divorce Celeste and marry her. Celeste countered with naming Rose as correspondent, and the newspapers had a field day with the scandal. But Charles gave in to the pressure and told the court that he had never had anything to do with Rose. Added to Rose's grief was the sudden death of her father. Then Rose found that she was pregnant and Rose's old friend Ellis Smith stepped in to the rescue.

Ellis Smith was a strange man. He was cynical, remote, and more than a bit of a mystery. In fact, the people of Five Points referred to him as "Mr. Nobody from Nowhere." He had never been in sympathy with Dr. Ruthledge's crusading, feeling that man was basically a selfish creature who masked his cowardliness with stupid, hypocritical philosophy. Ellis had been born into a wealthy family but rebelled against their extravagant ways. Ellis finally broke with his father over Ellis's dream of becoming a painter.

Reverend Ruthledge's Sermon
Armistice Day
November 11, 1937

Friends and neighbors, gathered here this evening are peoples of every nationality and creed, many of whom remember back nineteen years, when the Armistice was signed—the Armistice which brought to an end the Great World War. Many of you look back with heartache and with tears on what the World War did to your families—to your boys. It seems only yesterday that we stood on the streets and heard the chimes of the churches, the whistles of the factories, the cheering of the crowd, the long awaited words: The Armistice is signed—the war is over.

And then several months passed and the first transport bringing American soldiers landed in New York. And up and down Broadway we heard the marching of feet. And again we heard the bugle, not of war, but of peace. The cheers of the American public echoed and re-echoed "our boys are coming back home." What a gala holiday was celebrated! Emotions ran high—the strain was over—the war was over—the first American soldiers were again on their own soil.

For the time being, the American public did not remember that in many homes in the city and the country shone brightly the gold stars—stars that told us of the men—the boys—who would not—who could not come back— men and boys who had died on foreign soil. Each year on November eleventh at eleven o'clock in the morning we are asked to turn to the East and remember the men who did not come back.

Friends, there seems to be a word that has found its way into the consciousness of countries all over the world—a word which we know, just nineteen years ago, brought horror, destruction, agony to mankind—WAR. Hardly has the destruction of the last war been remedied before we have the foreboding—the indication—that there is likely to be another war before very long. Do we want another war? Can we afford another war?

As I have read the newspapers—as I have seen the newsreels showing the devastation in China—I have been hoping that the men who control the destiny of this great country of ours will have the courage to say to Europe—to Asia— if you insist on making war on each other, do not expect an ounce of American

The Reverend Doctor John Ruthledge (Arthur Peterson), 1937. (Author's Collection.)

grain—a dollar of American money—nor a man wearing an American army or navy uniform to set foot on foreign soil.

Do the men—will the men—who carry the destiny of your mothers and your fathers—of your homes and your families, in their hands—will they dare to set up America as an example of what a real armistice can and should mean? You young mothers, who are rocking your babies, singing them lullabies—do you know what is being planned while you dream of your son growing into manhood? There are those who are planning to make bigger and better airplanes—a flight of an airplane—a flight of death, not life.

You mothers and fathers who send your sons to school each morning—who are making plans for their futures—do you realize that this Armistice Day—there are those who are making uniforms and boots for soldiers to wear? Do you mothers and fathers realize as you hear the prayers of your boys—of your babies—that there are those who are testing chemicals to make deadly gas—to destroy that which you have brought into the world? Do you mothers and fathers realize that while you are trying to build sturdy, young bodies, that somewhere there are those who are waiting to again blow the bugle notes that call only those who are fit to be killed? You, who would build splendid men, strong, erect—do you know that there are those who are trying to produce more powerful guns—guns that may someday leave a golden star in your windows and bitter hatred in your souls?

Are we going to continue to observe the Armistice that was signed on November 11th, 1918—or are we going to be caught in the whirlpool of war madness? My friends, it's for you to answer that question.

After drifitng aimlessly for years, Ellis settled to live in virtual poverty in the town of Five Points. Gradually, he discovered that the town was not a community of parasites, but rather that the people were strong individualists who created their own destinies. Meeting Rose Kransky changed his life. Her zest for life fascinated him and he began painting again. When Rose fell for the oldest con game in the book, Ellis came forward and proposed marriage. Rose appreciated the offer, but bravely decided to bring up Johnny on her own. Complicating matters was the reintroduction of Charles Cunningham to Rose's life. After Charles ditched his wife, and the scandal subsided, Charles proposed that he and Rose marry. However, one week before the planned wedding, tragedy struck. One of Jacob Kransky's friends left the gate to the Kransky's yard ajar. Little Johnny wandered out into the street and was struck by a car and killed. Distraught, Rose called off the wedding—she didn't need Charles's nobility or pity—and vowed to make a new life for herself.

Afterwards, Ned's ex-wife Torchy came back to town and tried to strike up a relationship with Ellis, but Ellis was too preoccupied with other problems. He had received injuries in a disastrous fire and was left blind. Ellis's daughter, Nancy Stewart, an art student, the product of Ellis's marriage to a socialite years before in Chicago, had also popped up in town. Nancy had no idea that the mysterious Ellis was her father, and Ellis had no wish to reveal himself until she had learned to look upon him as a friend. For a while, the seemingly selfish Iris Marsh, a thirty-year-old rich divorcée, seemed very sympathetic to Ellis's plight. Coming from wealth, but unwilling to talk about her past, she was labelled "Miss Nobody from Nowhere." The two shared cultural tastes and quickly struck up an intimate friendship. The similarities between Ellis and

Guiding Light Milestones
Radio

1918.   Reverend Ruthledge moves to Five Points and opens his church
         to all.

1937.   Ned and Mary are engaged.
         Abe Kransky dies from influenza.

1938.   Fredrika shoots and kills Paul Holden.

1939.   Rose Kransky has child out of wedlock.

1941.   In June, Ned and Mary are finally wed.
         Johnny Kransky dies in an automobile accident.

1942.   Ellis Smith and Torchy Reynolds Holden marry.

1943.   Norma Greenman dies of a heart attack.

1945.   With Dr. Ruthledge overseas, Dr. Richard Gaylord becomes
         minister in Five Points.

1946.   Reverend Ruthledge dies.
         In July, Tim Lawrence dies in a plane crash.
         In October, Dr. Jonathan MacNeill marries Claire Lawrence.

1947.   Ray and Charlotte marry.
         Dr. Charles Matthews opens the Church of the Good Samaritan.

1948.   The Bauer family is introduced.
         Roger Collins marries Susan McClain

1949.   On December 9, Bert and Bill are married.
         Mama Bauer dies shortly afterwards.

1950.   On February 6, Meta and Ted marry.
          On September 20, Chuckie dies.
          On September 22, Meta shoots and kills Ted.

1951.   In April, Meta is vindicated in the Ted White case.
          On September 7, Meta marries Joe Roberts.
          Trudy Bauer marries Clyde Palmer.

Announcer Bud (Beat the Clock) *Collyer (far right) oversaw all the intrigue as Charlotte (Lesley Woods, far left) and Ray Brandon (Staats Cotsworth) supported Meta (Jone Allison) in her fight against Ted White, 1949.*

Iris made Torchy extremely jealous, and for a while Torchy dated Martin Kane, Torchy, and he embarked on a commendable campaign: organizing a Seeing Eye training group for returning war verterans who had lost their sight in overseas battles. After Nancy learned that she was Ellis's daughter, she put Ellis and Torchy through hell because of real and imagined slights. But Nancy eventually mellowed toward her father and Ellis was operated upon for his blindness and was cured. Eventually, he was reconciled with Nancy.

Rose went to work as governess for the two children of wealthy, unconventional Edward Greenman. Edward was not happy in his marriage to the unstable, possessive Norma. But he was content enough to continue his marriage, losing himself in his business. But when he saw the affection that Rose showered on his children—nurturing that Norma seemed incapable of—Edward found himself falling in love with Rose. Although Rose and Edward's relationship was platonic, Norma became violently jealous. The discovery that Norma's irrationality was due to a brain tumor brought nothing but unhappiness for Rose and Edward for some time to come. Norma underwent brain surgery, was cured, and tried to pull her life together, her jealously of Rose waning. Norma opened a nursery school, but one day a student was spotted drowning in a freezing lake, and Norma plunged into the icy waters to rescue the child. Afterwards, Norma contracted pneumonia and died of a heart attack the night after her release from the hospital.

Norma and Edward's fifteen-year-old daughter, Joan, could not accept her mother's death and blamed the entire mess on Edward and Rose. Reading her mother's diary, Joan became neurotically convinced that Edward had had Norma killed so he could marry Rose. Joan ran away to her grandparents, the Levines, to tell them her fears. Edward, feeling very guilty, burned the diary, making it seem that he had some culpability in Norma's death. With Edward's situation desperate, the Greenman's nurse admitted it was her irresponsibility that led to Norma's death. Quite ashamed of herself, Joan admitted her mistakes to Dr. Ruthledge, and Rose and Edward were eventually wed.

With the advent of World War II, Dr. Ruthledge went overseas to serve as a chaplain. Dr. Richard Gaylord, who married Peggy Lamont, became the new pastor, followed by the Reverend Frank Tuttle and his young assistant, Bill Brown. The ministers attempted to help Claire Marshall, whose life was in turmoil. Claire had married pilot Tim Lawrence and adopted a little boy. Ricki, who turned out to be the natural son of Tim from his unhappy first marriage to Nina. Then Tim was killed in an airplane crash. Claire turned to Dr. Jonathan MacNeill, who had loved her for some time. After their eventual marriage, Claire and Jonathan moved to Selby Flats, California.

Ned Holden arrived in Selby Flats, a suburb of Los Angeles, with the news that Dr. Ruthledge had passed away. Ned brought with him Dr. Ruthledge's lamp of friendship—the symbol of guiding light—and presented it to the Reverend Dr. Charles Matthews, an old friend of Dr. Ruthledge. Dr. Matthews lived with his sister Winifred Hale, and Winnie's daughter Pamela.

Dr. Matthews was friend and advisor to an ex-convict, Ray Brandon (*né* Roger Barton), who, justifiably, had a chip on his shoulder. The embezzlement for which Ray had been imprisoned had actually been committed by Martin McClain, Ray's employer, a wealthy businessman who had framed Ray. When Ray was sent to prison for fifteen years his wife Julie had divorced him and married Frank Collins. Ray's son Roger had even taken his stepfather's surname. Ray vowed revenge against Martin, but came to his senses just before pulling the trigger.

Ray was attracted to Charlotte Wilson, a singer, who lived at the same rooming house. Charlotte had a habit of running away from her problems, and her problems usually dealt with men. She had once been engaged to Larry Lawrence, brother of the late Tim Lawrence. Larry had suddenly shown up in Selby Flats and started giving Charlotte a hard time. Ray was also having problems with his ex-wife Julie, who although married to another, signaled her interest in Ray. But Charlotte and Ray finally realized their love for each other and married.

Julie's children, Betty and Michael, were tragically killed in a car crash, an accident that left Julie's husband Frank paralyzed from the waist down. Then Julie was accused of pushing Frank and his wheelchair off a cliff! Ray rushed to be at his ex-wife's side, and later Frank's death was ruled accidental. But Charlotte misunderstood Ray's sympathy for his ex-wife and moved out. By this time Charlotte was clearly torn between her marriage and career. Her agent Sid Harper, who was in love with her, encouraged her to work more, as did Ted White, a radio agency businessman who became professionally interested in promoting Charlotte.

At the Towers apartment building, Charlotte became friends with Mary Leland, a physician, and Jan Carter, a model. Jan, who was vague about her past, began dating the wealthy Ted White. In time, Jan and Ted began an affair, but Jan broke it off when Ted was two-timing her with a starlet. When Jan realized she was pregnant, she fled to New York and entered a convent.

Meanwhile, Dr. Matthews was helping Frederick Bauer deal with another crisis, the illness of his wife. Dr. Matthews suggested that Mary Leland be her physician. Mama Bauer had surgery, but there was no guarantee of a full recovery. Complicating Mama's recovery was her emotional well-being. Her daughter Meta had run away from home five years before, breaking Mama's heart. Papa Bauer blamed his strict upbringing for Meta's disappearance. In time, it became apparent that model Jan Carter and Meta Bauer were one and the same person!

While at the convent awaiting the birth of her child, Meta confided her past to the Mother Superior, and the good sister urged Meta to return home and try to make peace with her family. Meanwhile, Charlotte and Ray reconciled, and because Charlotte was unable to bear a child of her own, the couple planned to adopt. Meta was determined to put up her child for adoption, so Dr. Mary Leland, Meta's attending physician, arranged for Charlotte and Ray to be the adoptive parents, although she withheld this from Meta.

Charlotte and Ray were overjoyed when the baby boy came into their lives. They christened him Charles, named after Dr. Charles Matthews and Charlotte herself, and nicknamed him Chuckie. Later, Meta did return home and was reconciled with her family. Meta also renewed her friendship with Charlotte and eventually realized that Chuckie was, in fact, her own son. Feeling an overwhelming sense of maternal love, Meta instigated a custody suit against Charlotte and Ray and won custody of Chuckie.

Charlotte and Ray's marriage began collapsing. Charlotte sought relief in tranquilizers and, overdosing, was committed to a sanitarium. But through the help of her friend Mary Leland, Charlotte pulled through. She and Ray reached a new understanding and reconciled. They made plans to adopt another child, and soon little Penny Reynolds became a member of the family. Later, the Brandons adopted Penny's teenage brother and moved to the East Coast.

Meanwhile, Ted White, Chuckie's natural father, learned of Meta's custody win. Determined to have his son by his side, Ted made romantic overtures to Meta and tried to persuade her to marry him. Meta resisted, determined to raise Chuckie alone. Meta found the attentions of Dr. Ross Boling, a colleague of Mary Leland, far more intriguing. But Meta's sister Trudy also had feelings for Ross, and the Bauer home was filled with jealousy and tension. But two events soon brought the family together. Meta's brother Bill was married to the former Bertha Miller by the new pastor, Reverend Paul Keeler. A few days later, Mama Bauer passed away.

To give Chuckie a father, Meta finally gave in to Ted and married him, although she clearly did not love him. Meta became increasingly alarmed at the way Ted was treating Chuckie. He was trying to make a man out of a little six-year-old. Chuckie wanted to paint, but Ted took him on dangerous camping trips in the wilderness and forced Chuckie to take up swimming and boxing lessons. One day, Chuckie, sustained a skull fracture during boxing practice and was hospitalized. For an entire month, Chuckie hovered between life and death, and then tragically passed away.

Bert: Honey, I just want you to be on the alert. I know what you think of Ross, and given half a chance I know what he could think of you. Believe me, you have to fight for what you want. Take a few lessons from your sister Meta. She told me that she was going to take Chuckie for a checkup this afternoon. And I'll bet dollars to donuts that Dr. Boling checked him over.

Trudy: That's ridiculous—Ross isn't a pediatrician.

Bert: I don't think that would make any difference to Meta, do you? Honey, wake up. Don't let any grass grow under your feet. Assert yourself! You're Trudy Bauer—a very desirable young woman. You'd make Ross a wonderful wife. If he doesn't know it, you make it your business to let him know. And to be on the safe side, I'd tell Meta in no uncertain terms to keep her hands off! That's my advice to you.

Meta (Ellen Demming, right) fought an uphill battle with stepdaughter Kathy (Susan Douglas, left) who did not approve of Meta's marriage to her father, Joe Roberts (Herb Nelson).

Out of her mind with grief, Meta met up with Ted in their Beverly Hills home. She pulled out a gun, shot and killed Ted. For months afterwards, Meta could not remember the shooting and found herself continually drawn to the edge of a cliff, enshrouded in a heavy fog. She kept hearing Chuckie crying out for her to help him. Eventually, Meta was arrested for Ted's murder. At the trial, reporter Joe Roberts went along with the assumption that Meta had killed Ted in cold blood. But as he got to know her and became attracted to her, he came to believe Meta was innocent due to diminished capacity. The court agreed and Meta was cleared.

Joe and Meta fell in love, but because of Joe's children, teenager Kathy and young Joey, they kept their subsequent marriage a secret. When Joey fell ill with rheumatic fever, Peggy Regan was hired to be his live-in nurse. As Peggy fell in love with Joe, Kathy formed a close friendship with Peggy and hoped that her father and Peggy would get together. When Kathy learned of her father's secret marriage to Meta, Kathy was furious. Kathy's bitterness toward Meta soon caused a rift between Meta and Joe, and Meta went to New York. There Meta visited her sister Trudy, who had married Clyde Palmer after Trudy had gotten over her heartbreaking romance with Ross Boling.

When Meta returned to California, she and Joe reconciled. But Joe's daughter, Kathy, would cause years of heartache for the couple.

The Story on Television 5

Meta and Joe Roberts's marriage was strained from the start by Joe's trouble-some daughter Kathy; the resentful teenager couldn't believe that her place in the family was being usurped by such a scandalous woman. Fueling her self-destructiveness was her meeting the mother of Dick Grant, a young intern Kathy was in love with. The imperious Laura Grant greeted Kathy with outright hostility, and Kathy's dreams of marriage were shattered.

To spite Meta and her father, Kathy moved out, got a job in a department store, and, in one mad, impulsive moment, secretly married Bob Lang, a man she hardly knew. Shortly afterwards, Kathy realized her mistake: she had never stopped loving Dick. One night, while Bob and Kathy were driving home, Kathy admitted the truth and asked for a divorce. Bob was furious, began driving crazily and suddenly the car spun out of control. When Kathy regained consciousness, she felt for Bob's pulse and realized he was dead. In a daze, Kathy abandoned the wreck and later collapsed at a girl friend's apartment.

Kathy's girlfriend Alice convinced a guilt-ridden Kathy to keep quiet about her marriage to Bob and her involvement in the accident. That seemed the sensible thing to do especially since Dr. Dick Grant was back in her life and wanted to marry Kathy. One day, the pompous Laura Grant, dripping with venom, dropped in on Kathy and Meta. When Meta put the condescending Mrs. Grant in her place, Kathy felt everlasting gratitude and she and Meta became friends. Kathy confessed all to Meta—even the bombshell: she was pregnant with Bob Lang's child!

Bill Bauer (Lyle Sudrow, far right) attempted to intercede in the Roberts' family squabble. Kathy (Susan Douglas, right) deeply resented the marriage of her father, Joe (Herb Nelson) to Meta (Jone Allison), 1952.

Meanwhile, Meta tried valiantly to make a good home for Joe and his son, Joey (Tarry Green), 1952.

*Kathy briefly found
contentment with Dr. Dick
Grant (James Lipton),
1953.*

Despite Meta's plea for Kathy to be honest with Dick, an insecure Kathy went ahead and married Dick without telling him about her secret marriage, Bob's death, or her pregnancy. But an industrious newspaper reporter, finding Bob's death suspicious, dug up Kathy's marriage certificate. Because of her constant cover-up, Kathy was booked on suspicion of murder. The D.A. theorized that Kathy had murdered Bob to free herself to marry Dick, but Dick came forward and lied: he testified that he had always known about Kathy's marriage to Bob. Afterwards, the D.A.'s case fell apart.

Months later Kathy gave birth to a daughter, Robin. Guilt-ridden, Kathy became preoccupied with little Robin, leaving the door open for Nurse Janet Johnson to make a play for Dick. Sensing her marriage was shaky, Kathy sought counsel from the Reverend Dr. Keeler, who encouraged her to save her marriage by telling Dick about Robin's paternity. Kathy did so and her marriage was annulled. Impulsively, Kathy began dating Dick's roommate Dr. Jim Kelly, who soon proposed to her. Still in love with Kathy, angry with his roommate's intentions, and sick with hospital pressures, Dick "froze" one day at the operating table. Humiliated and despondent, he fled to New York.

Joe Roberts died from cancer which threw Kathy and Meta into an emotional tailspin; old resentments came flaring up. Kathy left Meta's side and took Robin to New York to try to make sense of her life. Months of grief followed for Meta, but her resilience and characteristic spirit returned. And when her brother Bill introduced her to business associate Mark Holden, Meta found herself falling in love. Unfortunately, Kathy returned to California and found *herself* being pursued by Mark! In the interim, Kathy had done a lot of growing up and refused to marry Mark until she was sure Meta would not be hurt.

In Mark, Meta felt the awakening of an all-consuming love. Her marriage to Joe had been steady and stable, perhaps too much so. She had been drawn to Joe's qualities—his untiring quest for justice, his love for his family. But it took Joe's death to open Meta's eyes to Mark, for whom she felt a true love, in

Meta (now played by Ellen Demming) weathered many a storm with the help of husband Joe, who died Christmas Eve, 1955.

June 16, 1958

Bruce: Meta, I'm the one who told you you were
         still in love with Mark. And if I hadn't
         said anything we'd probably be married. But
         it wouldn't have been any good. A woman
         can't be married to one man while she's in
         love with another one. At least not married
         to me.

Meta: I'm so confused—so mixed up.

Bruce: Then take some time to get un—confused.
         Learn to face your feelings. Meta, Mark
         Holden is free to get married again now. You
         owe it to yourself to see if Mark might feel
         some day the way you do.

Meta: Mark never felt about me as I did him.

Bruce: But as you said, there are all kinds of
         love. On the other hand, maybe things will
         never work out between you. Maybe someday
         you will stop loving Mark—and if you do—

Meta: Yes, Bruce?

Bruce: Well, if that time does come, darling, let
         me know. I'll probably still be around.

body and in soul. Eventually, Meta and Kathy both won—and lost—when it
came to Mark. After her experience with Mark, Meta was free to embark on
the most satisfying and least complicated marriage of her life—to Dr. Bruce
Banning, who had waited patiently for Meta to get over Mark.

Eventually, Kathy did marry Mark, but ironically history began repeating
itself: Kathy's daughter Robin resented Mark's intrusion into her protected life

Both Meta and Kathy fell in love with Mark Holden (Whitfield Connor), 1956.

Eventually, Meta married Dr. Bruce Banning (Les Damon, center), 1958. Their stable marriage was in marked contrast to Bert and Bill's.

much the way Kathy had resented Meta. Meta found herself in the awkward position of becoming a mother figure for the troubled Robin, who became more alienated from Kathy as time went on. Suddenly and tragically, Kathy was killed in an automobile accident. And it soon became apparent through her unusual behavior that Robin would follow in her mother's footsteps, growing up confused, frightened, and rebellious.

Meanwhile, in New York, Dr. Dick Grant met (at Mrs. Laurey's boarding house) artist Marie Wallace, who brought Dick out of his deep depression. Here was one woman to whom Dick's world of free-flowing money and exaggerated public importance was totally foreign. Dick was going under the assumed name Richard Edmunds, and Marie painted his portrait, entitled "Dark Echo." Afterwards, Dick and Marie returned to California, where Marie received treatment for an eye condition. Although Marie met with immediate disapproval by Dick's mother Laura, she and Dick were married.

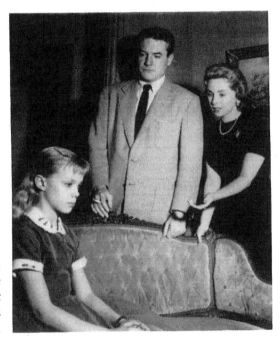

Kathy's marriage to Mark was threatened from the beginning by the resentment of her daughter, Robin (Zina Bethune), 1956.

Laura antagonized Marie for years to come. Dick and Marie's marital problems were compounded by Dick's sterility and his refusal, out of masculine pride, to adopt a child. Marie found herself the object of both fellow artist Joe Turino's affections and the backhanded manipulations of Dick's mother. Through a series of misunderstandings, Dick and Marie filed for divorce. Then, a young heart patient named Phillip Collins came into Dick and Marie's lives. Dick and Marie reconciled, adopted Phil, and moved to Europe, their life finally a happy one. Crushed, Joe began keeping company with the charming blueblooded, Amy Sinclair.

While Meta eventually found contentment in her life with her marriage to Dr. Bruce Banning, trouble brewed off and on for years between her brother Bill and his wife Bertha. His affair with singer Gloria LaRue early in their marriage was never quite forgotten—Bill had been at Gloria's side, developing a TV program for Gloria to star in, while Bert gave birth to their son, Michael.

Robin grew up confused, rebellious, 1958.

Guiding Light Milestones
The Fifties

1952   In March, Michael Bauer is born.
          Kathy marries Bob Lang.
          Bob Lang is killed in an automobile accident.
          Kathy marries Dick Grant.
1953.   In May, Kathy gives birth to Robin.
1954.   On New Year's Eve, Ed Bauer is born.
          Joey Roberts marries Lois.
1955.   On Christmas Eve, Joe Roberts dies.
1956.   Mike Bauer runs away from home.
          Dr. Jim Kelly and Lila Taylor are wed.
1957.   In February, Kathy marries Mark Holden.
          On March 14, Papa Bauer celebrates his sixty-fifth birthday.
          On May 31, Dick Grant and Marie Wallace are wed.
1958.   In March, Kathy is killed in an automobile accident.
1959.   Dr. Paul Fletcher and Anne Benedict are wed.
          Mark Holden marries Ruth Jannings.

Bert's constant complaints about lack of creature comforts and Bill's lack of initiative in his job with an advertising agency soon drove Bill into seeking solace from a bottle.

Bert would insist that Bill invest large amounts of money in risky, speculative ventures which, she believed, would one day earn them luxuries equal to their neighbors'. She even bought a mink stole on credit and put a down payment on a house behind Bill's back. Bert was too young and too self-absorbed to realize that the more she nagged Bill, the more aggravated his feelings of failure became.

Bill also resented Bert's naming their first son not William, after his father, but Michael; he felt Bert was punishing him for Gloria. For a while Bert and Bill compromised and nicknamed their son "Butch." Years later, when Bert gave birth to another son, Bill insisted that he be named William Edward Bauer, Jr., but when Bill Jr. grew up, he preferred being called Ed. Bill's life became one of pipe dreams, promising Bert a better life for their family, but he was a broken man, losing job after job and succumbing to alcoholism. Yet no matter how many times Bert left Bill, she realized that deep down she loved him and it was her responsibility to keep her sons' lives from falling apart.

When Bert's mother Elsie and her ailing second husband Albert Franklin moved in with the Bauers, young Michael's life suddenly seemed without foundation. Papa Bauer, who had always been there for Mike when his parents fought, moved out to live with Mike's aunt Meta. With his mother doting on his younger brother and with Grandma Elsie's constant barrage of criticism, Mike felt unloved and unwanted. The boy ran away from home and became

Young Mike Bauer (Glenn Walken) with his best pal, Papa Bauer (Theo Goetz), 1954.

Marie (Lynne Rogers), with husband Dr. Dick Grant (James Lipton, left), and his rival, Dr. Paul Fletcher (Bernard Grant).

Marie was also pursued by artist Joe Turino (Joseph Campanella), but he later fell in love with Amy Sinclair (Joanne Linville).

Bert and Bill in happier times, 1952.

lost. The Bauers became panic stricken over the next few days and a sketch, drawn by artist Marie Grant, appeared in the newspapers. When Mike was found, Bert became overprotective to the point of smothering the boy.

While Mike grew up under the thumb of the loving Bert, young Robin Holden grew up feeling more alone, adrift. In fact, the only time Robin felt secure and safe was visiting the Bauer family. So it seemed natural that the teenagers would be attracted to each other. The only problem was Bert, who was well aware of Robin's psychological problems and made no secret of her disapproval of any relationship Mike might strike up with Robin. Robin's dilemma was further intensified when her stepfather, Mark Holden, married his housekeeper Ruth Jannings. Ruth had a son, Karl, who fell in love with Robin.

Because Mike was a close friend of Karl's, Mike stepped out of the picture even though he and Robin still shared strong feelings for each other. Robin and Karl became engaged, but Robin came down with a mysterious illness which plagued her for months. After every conceivable test, Dr. Paul Fletcher could

<u>March 16, 1956</u>

Meta: Elsie, this is no time to argue, to get
            angry—

Elsie: Why shouldn't I be angry? You've just as
            much told me I don't love my own grandson.

Meta: Well, frankly, Elsie, I sometimes wonder if
            you know the meaning of the word love.

Elsie: Meta Roberts—you can say that to me—
            knowing what my life has been, what I've
            been through.

Meta: None of our lives has been easy, Elsie. I
            know what the loss of your husband meant to
            you. I lost my husband, too.

Elsie: I know you did, but you seem to have—

Meta: I seem to have *what*?

Elsie: I only meant—well, you're so much younger
            than I—

Meta: What has age got to do with it? I don't think
            I'd better hear what you meant, Elsie. But
            just remember this—I loved Joe Roberts
            with all my heart and soul!

Elsie: Uh, well, yes, I—

Meta: But now that he's gone, it doesn't mean I've
            lost my capacity to love. The love I had for
            Joe—I want it to work for other people. But
            I don't think you know how to do that,
            Elsie. You don't love anyone but yourself
            really.

Elsie: How can you say such a thing?

Meta: Because you—you upset a child's entire
          world.

Elsie: I—I!

Meta: Yes you did. I know what I'm talking about.
          Mike has spent many weekends with Papa and
          me, and I saw what was happening. I never
          thought it would come to this but—

Elsie: You think it's my fault, too, do you?

Meta: I know it's your fault, Elsie, and I only
          hope that Mike's running away will make you
          realize a few things. You've got a big job
          ahead of you, Elsie Miller, you've got to
          teach Michael how to love you, you've got to
          learn how to love him. You've got to learn—
          so many things.

CUT TO HOSPITAL ROOM AND MIKE'S SLEEPING FACE. HE HAS A
FEW BANDAGES ON HIS FACE WHERE HE'S BEEN SCRATCHED. WE
PULL BACK TO SEE PAPA JUST SITTING THERE BESIDE THE
BED. SUDDENLY MIKE STIRS, OPENS HIS EYES AND LETS OUT
AN UNEARTHLY SCREAM. PAPA LEANS OVER THE BED QUICKLY.

Papa: Michael! . . . Liebling! . . . Michael!

Mike: (SOME WHIMPERING AS HE FIGHTS THROUGH HIS
          FEARS. THEN SLOWLY HIS EYES FOCUS ON HIS
          GRANDFATHER.) Gr—Grandpa!

Papa: (REAL TEARS AS HE PUTS HIS ARMS AROUND THE
          BOY.) Ya, Michael . . . ya, ya . . .

PAN OVER TO THE DOOR AS BILL AND BERT ARE OPENING IT.
THEN FADE OUT.

not find any physiological reasons for Robin's illness. Then the seemingly abrupt Dr. Fletcher, who saw his own loneliness and insecurity mirrored in Robin, realized that her problems were psychological. He and Dr. Dick Grant theorized that her illness was due to an unconscious reluctance to marry Karl.

Just as Robin realized that she was still in love with Mike, Mike was making plans to take a job in Alaska to run away from facing his love for Robin, his best friend's fiancée. One afternoon, as Mike drove Robin to a fraternity picnic, Robin confessed that she couldn't marry Karl because she was still in love with Mike. Carried away by their emotions, Mike and Robin eloped and were married by a justice of the peace over the state line. When they returned, Mike told Karl about the marriage. Enraged, Karl attacked Mike and fell, hitting his head against an ornamental iron table. A few hours later, Karl died.

When it was learned that Mike and Robin were married on the afternoon

Bert and Meta toast Papa on his sixty-fifth birthday, 1957.

Bert and Bill's marriage was continually strained by his alcoholism, her impulsiveness, 1958.

of Karl's death, Mike was charged with voluntary manslaughter. But the coroner returned a verdict of accidental death and Mike was freed. Immediately afterwards, Bert insisted that Mike and Robin have their marriage annulled since Mike had lied about his age to get a marriage license. Realizing that Karl's death would always be between them, Mike fled to New York.

On the rebound, Robin became involved with Alex Bowden, the sardonic, powerful owner of Bowden art galleries. Although Alex was old enough to be her father, Robin welcomed the attention lavished on her by the famous Alex. Sensing her vulnerability, Alex pounced on Robin and pressured her to end her marriage to Mike and marry him.

Complicating Alex's plans was the entrance of his alcoholic ex-wife Doris Crandall, whose hope for a reconciliation with Alex was the only thing keeping her sober. Alex hired lawyer George Hayes to get Doris off his back, then took Robin to New York and so belittled Mike in Robin's presence that Mike agreed to an annulment. Embittered, Mike moved to South America, blaming his mother for his marital breakup.

<u>November 18, 1960</u>

Alex and Robin's First Encounter

Robin: Please go away. I don't need anyone to stay
          with me.

Alex: I mean it's pleasant to be the center of
          attention now and then, isn't it?

Robin: Go away.

Alex: Before you make a complete nuisance of
          yourself, I recommend you go home to your
          family.

Robin: I don't have any family—I don't have anyone
          anymore.

Alex: What a pitiful expression of abject self-
          indulgence. That's what's wrong with people
          today. They enjoy wallowing in what they
          like to consider great personal tragedy.
          Our little problem is always the most
          important thing in the world.

Robin: You don't know what you're talking about.

Alex: I know you are involved in some childish
          affair which you thought was the greatest
          romance since Romeo and Juliet. And now
          you've found out that your Romeo wishes to
          have your secret marriage annulled.

*Robin (now played by
Abigail Kellogg) found Alex
Bowden (Ernest Graves)
both fascinating and
annoying.*

*Dr. Paul Fletcher found
marriage to the wealthy
Anne Benedict (Joan Gray)
a happy one, despite the
interference from her father,
Henry.*

Mike Bauer (Gary Carpenter) fell in love with the exquisite but unstable Julie Conrad (Sandra Smith), 1962.

When Doris learned that Alex had married Robin, she fell off the wagon. Dr. Paul Fletcher, who had been treating Doris, further infuriated his wife Anne by continually coming to Doris's aid. Paul was a self-made man from the wrong side of the tracks, who had years before fallen in love with and married debutante Anne Benedict. Unfortunately, Anne's snobbish father Henry had always disapproved of the marriage, and when Paul left his prestigious job as chief of staff at Cedars Hospital to run a clinic in a run-down part of town, Anne partially shared her father's disgust.

Paul and Anne moved in over the clinic, but Anne never gave up her campaign to get Paul to abandon his idealistic struggle to keep up the failing clinic and to pursue a comfortable practice among high society. With gang violence erupting in the area, Anne, who feared for her and her son Johnny's safety, purchased a revolver. Both Anne and Robin, for various reasons, blamed Doris for troubles in their marriages. Recovering alcoholic Doris, stung by dual tongue-lashings, found a brandy bottle at the clinic and quickly drained it.

Anne discovered Doris pitifully drunk and threatening suicide with the clinic gun. As Anne lashed out at Doris, Paul arrived and lunged for the gun. The gun went off, Anne was hit and later died on the operating table. Guilt-ridden and in shock, Paul signed a confession and was put on trial for his wife's murder. But Doris, who had blacked out during the incident, finally recalled the details of the shooting and Paul was cleared.

Completely swept up by Paul Fletcher's trial was Mike Bauer, who went to work for George Hayes's law firm. Mike had returned from Venezuela to be at his mother's side during her cancer surgery. Bert recovered and she and Mike put aside some of their old differences. But Mike was a changed young man with a cavalier attitude toward life. When George Hayes's beautiful secretary Julie Conrad fell in love with Mike, the young man strung her along, though he still had feelings for Robin. When Robin and Alex Bowden divorced, she and Mike toyed with getting back together again, but decided just too much water had passed under the bridge.

When Julie told Mike she was pregnant, Mike told her to put the child up for adoption and he would pay the expenses. Appalled by Mike's behavior, the Bauers came together and applied pressure on Mike to marry Julie. Mike and Julie were married in Nevada by a justice of the peace. The marriage was stormy from the beginning. Julie couldn't shake her jealousy of Robin and was humiliated that everyone was well aware she and Mike "had" to get married. After giving birth to Hope, Julie felt that she was the family joke and made plans to divorce Mike and put her baby girl up for adoption. To put a stop to her plans, Mike finally told Julie that he had fallen in love with her.

Julie dutifully worked full time to help with Mike's law school education but had little faith in their troubled marriage. Finally she moved out, only to discover that she was pregnant again. Her confidant, Alex Bowden, proposed that Julie get a Mexican divorce and marry him. She accepted, then flung the news in Mike's face. Bert also discovered Julie was pregnant and told Mike, who assumed that the child was Alex's. Julie lost the baby and almost died. The truth came out about the pregnancy and a stunned Mike vowed to patch up their marriage.

Julie regained her strength physically but began to retreat from the world emotionally. She suffered a nervous breakdown, became suicidal, and received psychiatric help in a sanitarium. When Bert became obsessively overprotective of Hope, Mike moved to Philadelphia with Hope and found a nearby sanitarium for Julie. She eventually recovered, but their happy reconciliation was short-lived; Julie took ill and suddenly died. Mike moved to Bay City, Michigan, to begin a new life for himself and Hope.

Guiding Light Milestones

The Sixties

1960.   In February, Meta Roberts and Dr. Bruce Banning are wed.
          In July, Mike Bauer and Robin are secretly married.
          Hours later, Karl Jannings is killed in a struggle with Mike.

1961.   In June, Dick and Marie Grant drop their divorce plans and adopt
          Phil Collins.
          In August, Robin marries Alex Bowden.

1962.   In January, Bert's surgery for uterine cancer is declared a
          success.
          In October, Anne Fletcher is killed in an accidental shooting.

1963.   In May, Mike and Julie have a shotgun wedding.
          In September, Hope Bauer is born.

1964.   In April, Robin secretly marries Paul Fletcher in New York.

1965.   Mike Bauer graduates from Law School.
          Ed Bauer returns to Springfield to study surgery.
          Bill Bauer has affair with Maggie Scott.
          In July, Jane Fletcher and George Hayes are wed.

1966.   In February, Julie Bauer dies. Mike and Hope move to Bay City,
          Michigan.
          After years of sobriety, Bill Bauer drinks heavily for months. He
          finally joins A.A.
          In June, Jane Hayes gives birth to Amy.

1967.   In May, Ben Scott suffers a heart attack and dies.
          In September, Leslie Jackson and Ed Bauer are wed.
          In October, Robin is struck and killed by an automobile.

1968.   In March, Maggie Scott dies after unsuccessful surgery.
          In April, Mike Bauer returns to Springfield. He falls in love with
          his brother's wife, Leslie.

In September, Bill has a successful heart transplant.
In October, a pregnant Peggy Scott marries Marty Dillman, and
Johnny Fletcher marries Tracy Delmar (Charlotte Waring).
In December, Marty Dillman is murdered.

1969.   In March, Peggy gives birth to Billy.
In April, Ed's year-long drinking problem culminates in a drunken
driving arrest and a dismissal from the hospital staff.
In December, Johnny Fletcher and Peggy, as well as Sara
McIntyre and Lee Gantry, are married.

With two failed marriages behind her, Robin vacationed in Europe, then
took a job at Paul Fletcher's clinic. She soon discovered that there was much
more than a lifelong friendship between herself and Paul. When they began
dating, Paul's shy sister Jane balked, immediately sensing that Robin was a
threat to their family unit—Jane, her brother Paul, and his son, Johnny. Fueling
Jane's insecurity was her own bad luck with men: Dr. Peter Nelson had just
thrown her over and was also expressing an interest in Robin. Life was continually passing Jane by.

When Paul announced his wedding plans to Robin, Paul's young son
Johnny openly rebelled. His emotional outbursts, prompted by his aunt Jane,
so upset Robin that she fled to New York. Jane thwarted Paul's efforts to find
Robin, but George Hayes discovered Jane's manipulations and told Paul where
to find Robin. Paul and Robin were reunited and married, but kept their marriage secret until Johnny was ready to accept the idea of Robin as a stepmother.

Jane accidentally learned of the secret marriage and told Johnny that his
father had lied and betrayed them. Johnny, feeling totally rejected, ran away
from home, but was found a short time later at the Los Angeles Children's Zoo.
Paul angrily kicked Jane out of their house for what she had done. George
found Jane wandering dazed and confused outside and, in an effort to restrain
her, ran after her and was hit by a car. George underwent cranial surgery and
Jane snapped out of it.

Despite misgivings all around, Jane was accepted as George's nurse during
his recovery because of her special training. Jane nursed George back to health
and they found themselves falling in love. George realized the extent of Jane's

Robin (now played by
Nancy Malone) always
found refuge from crisis
with Papa Bauer.

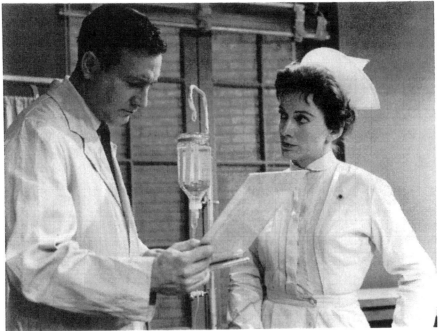

Spinster Jane Fletcher (Chase Crosley) was destructively overprotective of
her brother, Paul, 1965.

manipulations in the past and it caused problems for a while, but they eventually married. Some time afterwards, Jane gave birth to a baby girl, Amy.

Johnny's resentment toward his stepmother continued for years. He began spending time with his grandparents, Henry and Helene Benedict, in San Francisco. And when Grandma Helene was killed in an automobile accident, Johnny became more and more intransigent toward Paul and Robin. Henry Benedict began spoiling the young man and Johnny began to ape Henry's sophisticated ways, totally disagreeing with Paul's ideas about education, recreation, career, or money. The only person who could get through to Johnny was a new girl in town, Peggy Scott, whose honesty and lack of guile impressed Johnny.

Cleaning Johnny's room one day, a pregnant Robin fell off a chair and lost her baby. Robin's difficult recovery brought Paul and Johnny closer together. However, a depressed Robin became suddenly hostile toward Johnny because she felt he was inadvertently responsible for her miscarriage. She later made up with him but had a new problem to contend with. An old friend of Paul's,

Peggy Scott (Fran Myers, right) was the puppy-love girlfriend of Johnny Fletcher, stepson of Robin (now played by Gillian Spencer), 1965.

Dr. Sara McIntyre, had breezed into town, and Robin felt that there were indications that Paul and Sara's relationship exceeded the bounds of friendship.

Paul suggested that Robin see a psychiatrist, but the knowledge that Paul had once proposed marriage to Sara drove Robin to hysterics. She ran out onto a country road, was hit by a car, and died. The distraught motorist indicated Robin had thrown herself in front of the car, information that filled Paul with self-recrimination and despair. Three years later, after a half-hearted romance with Sara did not pan out, Paul took a leave of absence to work in Washington, D.C., and never returned.

The up-and-down marriage of Bill and Bert Bauer hit the skids when Bill became interested in his secretary Maggie Scott. One day, Maggie poured out her past to the sympathetic Bill, confessing that she had once been married to the disreputible Ben Scott, who had just popped into town. Maggie had married Ben against her parents' wishes when she was a high school senior and he was in the service. Her daughter Peggy, who was now a teenager, had been born while Ben was in Korea. When he returned to the States, Maggie realized that their marriage was a mistake, a diagnosis confirmed when Ben refused to obtain permanent employment, gambled, and was jailed for passing bad checks. After his disappearance, Maggie divorced him for desertion.

Ben Scott (Bernard Kates) and his estranged wife, Maggie (June Graham), have it out, 1965.

Maggie had tried to make a new life for Peggy and herself in the intervening fifteen years. But now Ben, suspiciously wealthy, had found Maggie and said that he had decided to settle down and make a home for her and Peggy. Maggie put Ben off, but Ben's reappearance was the answer to Peggy's many dreams of having her father back—shady past or not. Meanwhile, Bill's feelings for Maggie swelled as his domestic life deteriorated. Bert had become impossible to reason with when it came to their son Mike and their granddaughter, Hope. Bert's obsessive attention to Hope and her admonishments to Michael appalled him.

When Mike and Hope moved to Philadelphia, Bert was at loose ends. She and Bill fought constantly, and her second son, Ed, back home after medical school, virtually ignored her. Unbeknownst to Bert, Bill and Maggie began a guilt-ridden affair. Although hopelessly involved with Maggie, Bill became quite baffled as to what to do. He felt that he could not divorce Bert, the woman who had raised his family and stood by him through years of bad times. Bill's dilemma intensified when his son Ed lambasted him about the affair.

One day, Bert went to a restaurant and saw Bill and Maggie holding hands and engaging in an intimate conversation. A shocked Bert blamed herself because she felt that she had been neglecting Bill for years. With Papa Bauer's encouragement, she pulled herself together and decided to fight for her man. She went out and bought new clothes, went on a diet, and vowed to be more understanding. Meanwhile, Bill and Ed fought violently over Bill's affair, Ed demanding that Bill tell Bert about the affair before Ben Scott did. Bert, overhearing part of the argument, reprimanded Ed for being so disrespectful. Bert's actions reminded Bill of Bert's enormous love for him and Bill showed tenderness toward her for the first time in months.

Maggie decided to remarry Ben for two reasons: for her daughter's sake and because Ben held a love letter over her head that she had written to Bill, proving that she was an unfit mother. Depressed at Bert, Ed, and Maggie's unhappiness, Bill was persuaded by another executive, unaware that Bill was a recovering alcoholic, to have a few drinks to bolster his spirits. Bill succumbed and went on a drinking spree, the alcohol the only thing that made life bearable for him.

Ed ridiculed his father for his heavy drinking, realizing how it was hurting his mother—to say nothing of Ed's important career. Ed had met Leslie Jackson, a pretty young nurse's aide, who was the daughter of Dr. Steve Jackson, an eminent surgeon Ed was studying under. At first, career-minded Ed was rude to Leslie, but became attracted to her when he saw her loneliness. Little did Ed realize that Dr. Jackson was only advancing Ed's career because of his desire

June 7, 1966

Bert: Well, let me tell you something, young man,
           your father's not the only one who feels he's
           lost a son, I've lost a son, too. If you go on
           treating your father like this, we'll never
           get this family back together again!
Ed: I don't get this. My father turned his back
           on you, turned to another woman. Treated you
           the way no one should ever treat you, but you
           don't blame him for breaking up this home.
           You stand there defending him and you blame
           me for breaking it up.

Bert: I blame you because you're not loyal and
           decent enough to help put it together again!
           Thinking you're holier than he is. I just
           hope you're half the man your father is when
           you're his age. Your father's a big man, Ed,
           and you're small. It horrifies me to say
           this, but you're small.

Ed: You can stand there and tell me my father is a
           big man?

to have Ed marry Leslie. Leslie warned her father to butt out because she wanted to win Ed's attentions on her own terms. Watching all this coolly was Dr. Joe Werner, who knew the score and resented Ed's quick advances.

Ed became so down on the idea of marriage that he flatly told Leslie, "Why would anyone want to bring a child into a crazy, ugly, cockeyed world like this anyway." So Leslie, determined to forget Ed, began to date Joe Werner and later accepted his proposal of marriage. But when Dr. Jackson had to have heart surgery, Leslie began to depend more and more on Ed, who was assigned to the case. In time, Ed and Leslie rediscovered their feelings, but the jilted Joe vowed revenge. He began sabotaging Ed's work at the hospital, but Ed was cleared in every mishap, and Ed and Leslie finally married.

Bert: Yes, because he's a gentle man and a loving man and these are the only really good qualities there are in the world and I don't see them in you or you wouldn't treat your father this way. You may think you're superior to him but you'll never be fit to touch his boots!

Ed: I'm going to try to believe that you don't mean all of this. I didn't turn my back on my wife and turn to another woman; he did. I'm not out drinking in some bar now; he is. You're still so in love with him that you can't blame him for this, so you're trying to blame me.

Bert: Don't comfort yourself with that thought. I blame you for being the kind of boy who deserts his father in his hour of greatest need. And in deserting him, you've deserted me too. Yes, me too.

Ed's father Bill lost his job and tried again to put his life in order. He gave up drinking and tried to forget Maggie. Bert, getting a job as Paul Fletcher's secretary to support them—a blow to Bill's masculine pride—spurred Bill on, and after not taking a drink for six months, he found employment. Meanwhile, Maggie and Ben's loveless marriage continued. Ben, having his daughter Peggy at his side at last, was not about to lose her. When Ben discovered a budding romance between Peggy and Johnny Fletcher—a boy Ben saw himself in—Ben put an immediate stop to it.

During one of Bill Bauer's drinking benders, Bill told Peggy about his affair with her mother. Peggy was devastated. She and Johnny ran away to elope, but were involved in a car accident. At the hospital, a furious Ben told Johnny that Peggy, who was not seriously injured, was dying! Johnny then overheard some nurses talking about a young girl who had died, and he assumed that the dead girl was Peggy. Johnny took off for weeks, but eventually was told the truth, and he and Peggy were reunited.

Figuring Peggy would never forgive her for her affair, Maggie decided that she no longer had to endure the charade of her marriage to Ben. She divorced him and moved to New York. Going against Ben's wishes, Peggy on her eighteenth birthday went to get a marriage license for herself and Johnny. Ben went berserk, found Johnny at school, and beat him up. When Ben returned home, he collapsed, had a heart attack, and died. Peggy became withdrawn and rebuffed Johnny's overtures, telling him coolly that she did not want to get married to anyone for several years.

Shortly afterwards, Peggy's mother also died and Peggy moved in with the Bauers. While Tracy Delmar, a new girl in town, set her sights on Johnny Fletcher, Peggy became interested in Marty Dillman, a rich kid who asserted his masculinity by running around with a seedy crowd of hoodlums. Blocking out thoughts of Johnny, Peggy became pregnant with Marty's child and married Marty. Within weeks, Johnny married Tracy Delmar. When Marty was found dead with a fractured skull and a knife wound in the neck, Peggy was arrested

Bachelor Ed Bauer (Robert Gentry) met his match in the spunky Leslie Jackson (Lynne Adams), 1967.

The whole world seemed to be against the marriage of Peggy (Fran Myers) to Johnny Fletcher (Erik Howell), 1967.

for his murder. Peggy needed a good lawyer, so Bert called her son Mike to come home and defend Peggy.

Meanwhile, Tracy Delmar was unmasked as a fraud. She was not, as she claimed, Sara McIntyre's niece, but a gold digger from Oregon named Charlotte Waring. After Charlotte's marriage to Johnny was annulled. Charlotte came forward and testified that Flip Malone, Marty's grease monkey sidekick, had good reason to kill Marty. Flip confessed and Peggy was acquitted. Johnny and Peggy married and he adopted Peggy's little boy, Billy, named after Bill Bauer, whom Peggy had always looked up to. Impressed by Charlotte's bravery, Mike began to date her, but soon lost his heart to another woman.

Unfortunately, that other woman was married—to Mike's brother, Ed! When Mike had returned to town, he had offered Leslie brotherly support, and Leslie poured out her heart to Mike: Ed had problems at the hospital, had begun drinking under the pressure, and abused her at home. Mike urged Leslie to leave Ed, but she refused, feeling an obligation to stand by her husband. Soon, Mike and Leslie realized that they were falling in love, but Leslie was determined to help Ed get back on the track.

When Cedars Hospital suspended Ed because of his drinking, Ed came home and overheard Mike declare his love for Leslie. Something snapped inside Ed and he was overwhelmed by feelings of failure and inadequacy. He left Springfield for nearby Tarrywood, took an assumed name, and began working

Mike Bauer (now played by Don Stewart) returned to town with his daughter, Hope (Elissa Leeds), 1968.

in a factory, attempting to find a life where he could succeed at something. When Leslie put Mike off, Mike turned his attention to Charlotte Waring, who was more than willing to get her hooks into him.

In Tarrywood, Ed put his life in order. He found he got a great deal of satisfaction from working with his hands, moving warehouse stock. A secretary there, Janet Mason, took a liking to Ed and provided him with the emotional support he needed to join Alcoholics Anonymous. Ed finally realized that Janet was in love with him, so he told her the truth about his past. Ed couldn't promise Janet anything since he still wasn't sure who he was. Hurting another woman who only wanted to make him happy, Ed ran away, this time to Springfield to try to untangle his life.

When Ed returned, Leslie was deeply moved by Ed's tearful apology and agreed with her father that Ed should stay with her until he could rebuild his once promising surgical career. Mike was furious with the charade, but Leslie begged Mike to be patient. Ed needed as much support as possible now, especially since his father Bill was reported missing in a plane crash and presumed dead. At last the day came for Ed to perform surgery again. Everything went like clockwork, and Ed took Leslie out to celebrate. Ed thanked Leslie for her support and she felt a swell of pride inside her that grew stronger through the

<u>July 17, 1969</u>

Papa: We both know that you are trying to protect Ed's marriage. Only forgive me if I remind you—you are Michael's mother, too.

Bert: I know I'm Michael's mother. However, Ed is the son who needs me now. Not Michael. Ed's trouble is a matter of life and death. You and Bill don't seem to realize that. Moreover, it is Michael—yes, and Leslie too—they're both at the bottom of this. Ed just doesn't have a drinking problem. His brother, Michael, is trying to steal his *wife*.

Papa: Now, Bertha, Bertha—

Bert: When I think of the nights I spent praying that Ed would come home again. Now the thought of his coming home—frightens me so that I can't breathe sometimes—

Papa: You are afraid of what would happen if he found out that Leslie and Michael were in love with each other.

Bert: He *knows* they're in love! That's why he drank the way he did. What's more, I believe Ed would go back to drinking again—if indeed he has stopped now.

Papa: You don't think he's stopped?

Bert: I *did* think so. Now I'm not so sure. After I found out—what Michael and Leslie—mean to each other—especially when I had no *idea* of it—Well, now I'm not sure of anything anymore. Except one thing. I'll never forgive either one of them.

evening. Swept up in a wave of good feelings, the night ended with Ed and Leslie spontaneously making love.

Afterwards, both Leslie and Ed were confused. Was this what either of them really wanted? Adding to Ed's confusion was the reentrance into his life of Janet Mason. Ed realized that he wanted to give Leslie her freedom so he could be with Janet. But before Ed could tell Leslie, Leslie had some news for Ed—she was pregnant! Subsequently, Ed and Leslie decided to stay together for the child's sake. Mike was devastated over the news and sarcastically wished Leslie good luck. Then Mike whisked Charlotte Waring off to the wild weekend that she'd wanted for so long, and when they returned, the two were Mr. and Mrs. Michael Bauer!

Ed meant to forget all about Janet, but he couldn't get her out of his head. Janet had a new boyfriend, lawyer Ken Norris, but she put Ken off, still having

One of Hope's best friends was Christy Rogers (Ariane Munker—who later had memorable roles on a half-dozen other soaps).

Leslie got fed up with the Bauer brothers and married Stanley Norris (Michael Higgins), 1970. She was later tried for his murder.

feelings for Ed. Janet and Ed began secretly meeting. Soon after little Frederick was born—named after his great-grandfather Papa Bauer—Leslie found out that Ed was seeing Janet, and Leslie's years of sacrificing herself for other people exploded into rage. At last, Leslie realized that she belonged with Mike. But Mike was having a high old time with the hot-to-trot Charlotte, and Leslie was soon greeted with the same rude shock Mike had gotten from her—Charlotte was pregnant!

Charlotte didn't look forward to motherhood; she just wanted to have fun. At least mother-in-law Bert was around to do all the housework and take care of little Hope, who Charlotte perceived as a mere inconvenience. Bert soon became fed up with this witch who wouldn't lift a dustcloth to save her life, but Mike doted on Charlotte, so Bert continued to roll out the red carpet— which Charlotte promptly tracked mud on. Meanwhile, Leslie was completely lost. After her divorce from Ed, she dated Ken's father, Stanley Norris, a fortyish millionaire who made her laugh and gave her expensive gifts that made her feel important. Although Bert and her father told Leslie that Stanley was all wrong for her, Leslie no longer trusted either one of them. After a brief court- ship, she married Stanley.

Leslie was even more unprepared for her second marriage than her first. Stanley had three grown children: Ken, a young lawyer in the D.A.'s office, who was still romancing Janet Mason; Holly, an immature, insecure twenty-year- old dazzled by the father she had never known; and Andy, who was away serving in Vietnam. Leslie held out her hand in friendship to her stepchildren, who were actually her own age, and Ken Norris almost bit it off. Ken resented his father's new young honey, and told Leslie he wasn't Stanley's first young wife and she wouldn't be his last! Soon, Leslie realized Ken was right. Stanley was obsessed with power and women, so if Leslie lavished any attention on her son Freddy, Stanley bitterly resented it.

One night Stanley was found shot to death. Ken concluded that Stanley's unhappy new wife had shot him when she found out how ruthless and unfaithful Stanley really was. Leslie had been seen hysterically confronting Stanley with a gun in her hand. Leslie was indicted for Stanley's murder and Mike Bauer rushed to her side.

Mike found a list of suspects almost as long as the Springfield phone book. There was Linell Conway, Stanley's longtime secretary/mistress, who had become oh-so-tired of waiting to be the next Mrs. Norris. Then there was Barbara Norris, Stanley's first wife, still bitter about her husband's abandoning her and her children. There was also handsome but shifty employee Roger Thorpe, who had been promised a big promotion if he could bring Stanley's daughter Holly and her stock shares into line. Then there was Holly herself, who was furious with her father "pimping" for her. Finally, there was the rather strange Kit Vested, another of Stanley's young ex-wives.

Mike's sleuthing uncovered the suspects one by one, but they all proved to have airtight alibis—except, of course, Leslie. Linell Conway, on the witness stand, confessed that Stanley had fired her the day he was shot. Then Linell's mother Marion leapt to her feet and vented her fury at the dead man: Stanley had taken the best years of Linell's life, then dumped her. Marion had only meant to scare Stanley with the gun; instead the gun accidentally went off and Stanley was killed. Leslie was acquitted.

Although Mike and Leslie had grown closer during the trial, Mike seemed more devoted than ever to Charlotte. So Leslie decided to take a long vacation to plan a future without the man she truly loved. Meanwhile, when Charlotte had an accident and lost her baby, she was secretly relieved and played the grieving mother for months. Bert caught on to Charlotte's manipulations, and when the neglected Hope ran out in a snowstorm and almost died from frostbite, Charlotte tried to blame the whole thing on Hope. This opened Mike's eyes to Charlotte's insensitivity and he eventually filed for a divorce. Mike searched for Leslie but Leslie's father Steve, sickened by Mike's weakness in the Charlotte affair, refused to help him in any way. Mike resolved to wait for her.

Stanley Norris's children remained in Springfield. Ken proposed marriage to Janet Mason and Janet accepted, hoping to find warmth and security. But Ken began to doubt Janet's love—it appeared that she never had gotten Ed

Bauer out of her system. Janet's dilemma was magnified when another male admirer came into the picture. Roger Thorpe, who had an off-again, on-again relationship with Ken's sister Holly, began to hit on Janet. But Janet fended off his advances. Holly saw Roger coming out of Janet's apartment building, wiping lipstick off his face. Traumatized, Holly rushed out into the street and was hit by a car.

Ken found Roger's gloves in the apartment and exploded in a jealous rage. Roger came forward and admitted that he had made all the overtures and Janet had been totally loyal to Ken. Ken begged for Janet's forgiveness, which Janet eventually granted, but not before crying on Ed Bauer's shoulder. Meanwhile, Holly remained in the hospital, unable to walk. Ed Bauer suspected depression and took a special interest in her case, telling Holly how his own feelings of worthlessness had contributed to his alcoholism. Inspired by Ed, Holly did walk again, and the two began to date—although Ed was still secretly meeting with his old flame, Janet.

Janet found that she was pregnant with Ken's child and was finally reconciled with Ken. On the rebound, Ed went out and got smashed in the company of Holly. Impulsively, they got married the same night, but the next day an apologetic Ed suggested they get an annulment. Crushed, Holly lied, saying that an annulment was impossible because they had consummated the marriage. Ed had been too drunk to remember otherwise, so he tried his best to make this farce of a marriage work.

Meanwhile, Mike Bauer was shot by Flip Malone, the very same thug Charlotte had sent up the river for the Dillman murder. Leslie heard about the shooting and rushed to be at Mike's side. She promised to stand by Mike and proudly fight for their love. But it soon became clear that a major obstacle was in their way: Mike's estranged wife, Charlotte. The bitchy Charlotte tried every trick in the book to keep Mike under wraps, but none of it worked. Mike was granted his divorce, but when Leslie announced that she and Mike were going to be married, Leslie's father—who had been opposed to the relationship from the beginning—keeled over with a heart attack. Leslie, the dutiful daughter, told Mike that she wanted to nurse her father back to health before marriage could be considered. Mike, finally certain of Leslie's love, agreed to wait.

Mike's law partner Ken Norris was not so sure about his wife, Janet, who had resumed her close but platonic friendship with Mike's brother Ed. Janet developed severe back pains during her pregnancy and often consulted Ed for medical advice. In the midst of a snowstorm, Janet visited Ed and went into labor. Ed delivered Janet's baby girl, who was named Emily. Ken's jealousy grew when baby Emily's health problems brought Ed and Janet closer together.

Dr. Sara McIntyre (Millette Alexander, center) was easy prey for her nasty husband, Lee Gantry (Ray Fulmer), and his sidekick, Miss Foss (Jan Sterling), 1970.

One of Sara's suitors afterwards was Dr. Wilson Frost (Jack Betts), 1973.

Sara again was victim to foul play when the psychotic Kit Vested (Nancy Addison, center) kidnapped Sara's husband, Dr. Joe Werner (Anthony Call), 1974.

Ken's jealousy became so severe that Janet feared that he might become violent and moved out of the house. Ken realized that he needed help and began seeing a psychiatrist.

Another woman who had trouble with a psychotic husband was Dr. Sara McIntyre. Her new husband, Lee Gantry, planned to murder Sara for Sara's inheritance. But Mike Bauer helped expose Lee and his blackmailing housekeeper, Mildred Foss. Gantry murdered Foss in his creepy attic and, on a later occasion, tumbled from the attic window to his death while trying to murder Sara. Sara later married Dr. Joe Werner, once a young hothead and bitter rival of Ed for Leslie's affections. Joe had mellowed through the years, but his restlessness soon caught up with him. He was very sympathetic to Charlotte Bauer during Charlotte's messy divorce from Mike. Joe and Charlotte had dated years before and Charlotte ended up seducing Joe. Joe, feeling very guilty, broke it off but not before Charlotte's friend Kit Vested saw them smooching in the hospital parking lot.

Kit was a disturbed woman who had confided to Charlotte that she, Kit, was madly in love with Joe. When Kit saw Charlotte and Joe together, Kit's mind snapped and she planned revenge. Kit invited Charlotte over, served her a drink which was laced with barbiturates, and called Joe, saying that Charlotte had fallen and hit her head. Joe treated Charlotte for a concussion, but Charlotte died from a drug overdose, and the autopsy proved embarassing for Joe with his fellow doctors at Cedars. Joe assumed Charlotte's death was a suicide and felt great remorse. The board at Cedars removed Joe as chief of staff and Joe left town and began drinking heavily.

Mike and Leslie were finally wed in 1973. Joining the festivities, from left to right: Dr. Joe Werner (Anthony Call), Dr. Sara McIntyre (Millette Alexander), Ken Norris (Roger Newman), Janet Norris (Caroline McWilliams), the minister (Donald Bishop), Ed Bauer (Mart Hulswit), Holly Norris (Lynn Deerfield), Leslie (for two years played by Barbara Rodell), Mike (Don Stewart), Freddy Bauer (Gary Hannoch), Dr. Steve Jackson (Stefan Schnabel), Peggy (Fran Myers), Meta Banning (Ellen Demming), Bert Bauer (Charita Bauer), and Hope Bauer (Elissa Leeds). (Al Rosenberg/Sterling's Magazines.)

Kit found Joe and whisked him off to a cabin in the woods, cutting off all communication between Joe and his wife, Sara. With Kit manipulating the scenario, Joe filed for a divorce from Sara who, suspecting foul play, demanded a face to face meeting. Frantic, Kit tried to murder Sara with the same overdose she had given Charlotte, but Joe found them in time to save Sara. Kit pulled out a gun and wounded Joe, but in the subsequent struggle the gun went off and Kit was killed. Joe and Sara reconciled.

Another couple together after a long wait were Mike and Leslie, who had finally convinced Leslie's father Steve that Leslie and Mike were right for each other. Bert hosted the wedding at her home, and the whole extended Bauer family turned out, including Meta and Bruce, Sara and Joe, Peggy, Ken, and Janet, and even Ed and Holly. It was a wonderful day of reconciliation for the family, but they were soon plunged into a new era of domestic conflict.

Soon after the wedding, Mike's daughter Hope left for boarding school and Leslie's long-lost mother arrived on the scene. This was a shock to Leslie, who had been told her mother was dead, but Victoria Jackson Ballinger had plenty of surprises up her sleeve. Actually, Victoria had deserted Steve and Leslie when Leslie was still an infant. But Victoria soon charmed her daughter and ex-husband, and Steve loaned Victoria several thousand dollars supposedly to open a flower shop in London. Victoria was, in fact, using the money to pay for her longtime lover Alex's psychiatric treatments.

Alex did improve for a while, but then had a severe setback, so Victoria returned to Springfield to milk more money from Steve, quite unaware that Leslie and Mike were on their way to London to surprise Victoria. Mike and Leslie discovered Victoria's deception and when they returned they found Victoria romancing Steve, who had found his old feelings for Victoria awakened. Crushed by Victoria's lies, Steve threw her out of his life once again. But before she left, Victoria spitefully told Leslie that Steve was not Leslie's natural father. Leslie thought her mother was a great liar, but Steve confirmed that for once Victoria was telling the truth. Stunned, Leslie wondered if she could ever have anything more to do with the man she had adored as her father all her life.

Ken Norris was also stunned when his psychiatrist told him he needed to make major changes in his life. His own worst enemy, Ken quit therapy and began dictating his problems, which he blamed on Ed Bauer's attraction to his wife, into a tape recorder. Increasingly unable to distinguish fantasy from reality, Ken told Janet that his doctor thought he would improve faster if Janet moved back home. Janet agreed to a separate bedroom arrangement and hoped Ken would change, but Ken kept throwing tantrums. When Janet consulted Ken's psychiatrist, she was told Ken had stopped therapy months before.

Guiding Light Milestones
The Seventies

1970.   In April, Charlotte Waring and Mike Bauer are married.
In August, Frederick Bauer is born to Leslie and Ed.
In December, Lee Gantry is killed when he falls through an attic window.
On New Year's Eve, Sara McIntyre and Joe Werner are wed.

1971.   On July 2, Leslie Bauer and Stanley Norris are married.
In September, Stanley is murdered.

1972.   In March, Janet Mason marries Ken Norris.
In August, Johnny Fletcher suffers a nervous breakdown.

1973.   In February, Papa Bauer dies in his sleep.
In May, a drunken Ed Bauer marries Holly Norris in Las Vegas.
In June, Mike Bauer and Leslie are finally wed in a garden ceremony at Bert's home.
In August, Kit Vested murders Charlotte Bauer with an overdose of barbiturates.

1974.   In April, Kit Vested is killed in a struggle with Joe Werner.

1975.   In April, a berserk Ken Norris shoots Ed.
In July, Holly gives birth to Christina.

1976.   In February, Roger Thorpe and Peggy Fletcher are wed.
In June, Leslie is struck and killed by a car driven by Spence Jeffers.
In July, Holly and Ed are divorced.
In October, Malcolm Granger dies under suspicious circumstances.
In November, Joe Werner dies.

1977.   In April, Rita is acquitted in the Malcom Granger murder trial.
In September, Bill Bauer "returns from the dead."
In November, the Spaulding family moves to Springfield.

1978.   In May, Ben McFarren and Eve Stapleton, as well as Sara McIntyre and Dean Blackford, are married.
In September, Amanda is married to Gordon Middleton.
In October, Roger rapes Rita.
In November, Ed Bauer and Rita are finally wed.

1979.   In January, Roger Thorpe marries Holly.
         In January, Dean Blackford is killed after a nasty spill.
         In February, Alan Spaulding marries Jackie Marler.
         In March, Roger rapes Holly.
         In June, Holly shoots Roger.
         In September, Brandon Spaulding dies.
         In October, Justin Marler marries Elizabeth Spaulding.

Driving home, Janet argued with Ken so violently that she lost control of the steering wheel and the car crashed. Ken was blinded in the accident and moved in with his mother Barbara and new stepfather Adam Thorpe. Barbara tried to be supportive of her son, but Ken became bitter and hostile, refusing to take classes to learn to cope with his blindness. Barbara also had her daughter Holly to contend with. Holly complained continuously about Ed's long hours at the hospital and was uneasy with Ed's ongoing friendship with Janet. Adam consoled Barbara about her children, reminding her of all the mistakes he had made with his son Roger.

Roger Thorpe moved back to Springfield and in with Adam and Barbara. Roger seemed to have mellowed and told his father and Barbara that he was ready to settle down and start a family. Impressed with Roger, Barbara spoke well of him to Holly, completely unaware that she was feeding Holly's fantasies of how exciting Roger was and still might be. Roger began dating Peggy Fletcher, who was separated from her husband Johnny after Johnny had nearly suffered a breakdown and left town. Peggy and Roger enjoyed their outings together, and Roger became fond of Peggy's young son Billy. So Peggy soon disregarded Holly's warnings of how untrustworthy Roger was.

But it turned out that Holly was the untrustworthy one. She took to hanging around Roger telling him how wrong he was for Peggy and how bored he would be with her. Roger was amused by Holly's attentions, but kept her at arm's length. That is, until Peggy began backing away from Roger, saying she couldn't commit herself to Roger while still legally married to Johnny. At the same time, Roger's business began to fail and he borrowed from loan sharks to keep it going. These setbacks made Roger very insecure and vulnerable to Holly's flirtations. One afternoon, Holly told Roger that he would never fit in in Springfield and Roger teased her that she was jealous of Peggy and still wanted him. Holly denied it, but Roger kissed her and she kissed him back just as passionately, and they fell into bed. Afterwards, they both said it wouldn't happen again, but it did—again and again.

Meanwhile, Peggy had reconciled herself to the fact that her marriage to Johnny was over. When Peggy told Roger that she had filed for a divorce, Roger was thrilled and immediately proposed marriage. Peggy put all her fears aside and accepted. So, Roger resolved once and for all to grow up, telling Holly that they could only be friends. Ed noticed Roger and Holly's friendship and was noticeably jealous. It was then that Holly realized that her marriage to Ed could be saved if only she used a little initiative. But her plans were temporarily stymied when she learned that she was pregnant—with Roger's child! Undaunted, Holly seduced her inattentive husband and soon afterwards announced her pregnancy to an ecstatic Ed.

Suddenly, Roger's new life with Peggy seemed lost forever. When he was late with a payment, the loan sharks had Roger badly beaten and threatened Peggy and Billy. Peggy had awful flashbacks to her teenage marriage to the notorious Marty Dillman, and feeling that she had to protect Billy from the thugs, Peggy broke up with Roger. Roger was saved from further violence when Holly used most of her inheritance to bail Roger out with the sharks. Everyone, including Ed, was impressed by Holly's "generosity," never suspecting that Holly was again fantasizing about a life with Roger.

Holly's brother Ken recovered his sight, but his pathetic attempts to win Janet back failed miserably. Ken's resentment of Ed grew to pathological proportions and Ken even faked a suicide to garner sympathy. When Ken caught Ed in an innocent embrace with Janet, he went berserk. He bought a gun and shot Ed in the chest. Ed was rushed into surgery and Joe Werner operated on a severed pulmonary vein, which left Ed's left hand partially paralyzed. Afterwards, Janet was so overwhelmed with guilt that she took baby Emily and moved to San Diego. Ken was placed in a sanitarium.

Suffering a severe depression after his operation, Ed only snapped out of the doldrums by the prospect of Holly giving birth to "their" child. Meanwhile, Holly had so many conflicting emotions to deal with, she hardly knew whether she was coming or going. She was wracked with guilt because of Ed on the one hand, but her obsession with Roger continued and she was perversely fascinated by Roger's renewed relationship with Peggy Fletcher. Holly was able to confide in her brother Andy, who had just returned to Springfield. Andy, a writer, tried to be supportive, but was intrigued by the idea of an illicit pregnancy and began a book, *Valerie's Story*, based on Holly's life.

Holly went into labor and delivered a girl, who was named Christina. The "premature" Christina soon became ill after birth and needed a blood trans-

Ed's marriage to the neurotic Holly Norris (Maureen Garrett) seemed doomed from the start, 1976.

fusion. Holly couldn't donate because of childhood hepatitis and Ed's blood was not the right type, so Roger donated the blood anonymously and Christina's life was saved. The months of terror and deceit finally got to Holly and she poured out the entire ugly story to Ed about her affair with Roger. Ed was disgusted, walked out on her, and told Roger he had exactly two weeks to tell Peggy the truth or Ed would. Instead of whisking Peggy off to get married, Roger confessed all. It took some time for Peggy to forgive him, but they were eventually married in a small ceremony with only Adam Thorpe and Bert Bauer in attendance.

Mike Bauer wasn't sure what to make of it when his daughter Hope wrote from college that she was involved with one of her professors, Alex McDaniels. When Hope came home on a visit and explained that, while Professor McDaniels was married, he and Hope planned to be wed once his divorce came through. Mike exploded and went to McDaniels and found the absent-minded professor carrying on with his wife! Threatening Alex with exposure and a morals charge,

February 3, 1976

(Emmy–Award–Nominated Script)

Roger: Peggy–nothing's changed in my feeling
        about you. You know that, don't you?

Peggy: I–guess so.

Roger: I hope so. And–this may sound strange to
        you but whatever happens from now on, if I
        ever amount to anything, or achieve
        anything–it's all for you. I'll be
        thinking of you.

Peggy: Roger–

Roger: I've caused so much trouble and unhappiness
        for you and Billy. There's only one thing I
        can do. Get out of your lives.

Peggy: What do you mean?

Roger: I'm going to leave Springfield.

Peggy: Because of me?

Roger: I've hurt other people. Too many of them.
        But hurting you is more than I can stand.
        So, there just isn't any other choice. I
        have to get out. Don't you see that?

Peggy: Roger–

Roger: Thanks for–being you.

Mike forced Alex to break off with Hope. Subsequently, Hope, furious with her father's interference, moved in with grandmother Bert.

Mike was also concerned with Leslie's renewed acquaintance with her old high school sweetheart, Chad Richards, a singer. Chad suffered from blackouts which worried both Leslie and Hope, who had begun working in the nightclub Chad performed in. Leslie's father ran tests which indicated a brain tumor, but Chad was terrified of surgery. One night, Chad attacked Leslie during a blackout and only Mike's fortunate arrival saved Leslie from serious injury. Chad was rushed into emergency surgery and a benign brain tumor was located and removed. After his recovery, Chad was too ashamed to remain in town, so he left Springfield.

Meanwhile, Ed Bauer was preparing to take one terrific tumble off the wagon. Steve Jackson had performed surgery on his hand, but there was too much scar tissue and it was thought that Ed could never perform surgery again. Ed struggled with the loss of his marriage and his career, but he did attract the attention of a sexy new nurse, Rita Stapleton. Rita dated a lot of guys, including Tim Ryan, which put the brakes on Tim's slowly developing relationship with Pam Chandler. But Rita noticed that Ed had the kind of warmth and stability she had always craved—and his income wasn't half bad, either.

Mike's overprotectiveness rubbed Leslie (once again, Lynne Adams) the wrong way, 1975.

Turning away from Holly, Ed found the attentions of Rita Stapleton (Lenore Kasdorf) most appealing, 1976.

Ed was receptive to Rita's friendship and began confiding in her. Rita was dismayed at the extent of Ed's problems and she continued seeing other men, especially Tim Ryan. But as the months wore on, Ed decided that his marriage to Holly couldn't possibly work and he admitted to Rita that he cared for her. As a gesture of good faith, Rita dropped Tim Ryan, who had fallen deeply in love with her—to the extent of neglecting his duties at the hospital. Pam found that she could not fill the void in Tim's life, as did Rita's younger sister Eve, who also cared for Tim. Pam eventually left Springfield to try to reconcile with baby Samantha's father.

Tim left too, but not before Eve demanded an explanation and Tim confessed his obsession for Rita. Eve blamed Rita for leading Tim on and accused her sister of needing to play with several men's affections at once for her own amusement. The sisters, however, were reconciled when their mother Viola was stricken with a brain tumor. Ed's speedy diagnosis pinpointed the exact spot where the delicate surgery should take place. Overwhelmed with emotion, Rita told Ed that she loved him, then almost took it back—until Ed smiled and told Rita he felt the same way. Ed's divorce from Holly was coming through. However, at the last minute, Holly had a change of heart and tried to reach Ed; but Rita made sure Ed never got the message. A depressed Holly took off for Europe for a long vacation.

Holly's mother Barbara's marriage became strained when Barbara found Andy's manuscript, *Valerie's Story*. Barbara realized it was really Holly's story and began to resent Roger to such an extent that she began suffering migraines. She couldn't confide in her husband—Adam was Roger's father. On the verge of a breakdown, Barbara spewed out all her hostile feelings toward Roger. Adam tried to reasonably answer Barbara, and even Holly tried to intercede, but Barbara could not shake her bitterness toward Roger. Her relationship with Adam was never quite the same and the two eventually divorced.

Another once-happy couple experiencing marital problems were Mike and Leslie. Now that Freddy was no longer a toddler, Leslie decided that she wanted to go back to college. Mike was not crazy about the idea and pointed out that she would feel out of place and her homework would certainly interfere with their social life. Besides, what would she do with a degree anyway? Leslie reminded Mike that she had put her own education aside for many years because of the men in her life, and now she wanted to do something for herself. Male chauvinist Mike eventually saw the light and Leslie greatly enjoyed her classes.

Mike was also unhappy about daughter Hope dating Mike's former client, artist Ben McFarren. Ben talked Hope into posing nude for his art class, then seduced her. Mike warned Hope that Ben was a convicted thief and would end up hurting her. But Ben proposed and Hope accepted. Shortly afterwards, Ben's brother Jerry, who had actually committed the robbery Ben was sent to prison for, borrowed Ben's car and robbed a deli. The car was traced to Ben, who was arrested. Ben withdrew most of his savings account to repay the deli owner, who believed Ben's story about Ben's brother and dropped the charges. Unfortunately, Hope could not bring herself to trust Ben and broke off their relationship.

Putting various domestic crises behind him, Mike concentrated his energies on a new client, Ann Jeffers. Ann told Mike that her husband Spence had kidnapped their son Jimmy several years ago and she had been searching for them ever since. Mike took a special interest in her case and accompanied Ann on several trips to California where they finally located Spence. Spence had remarried and claimed that Jimmy had died years before. Mike didn't believe

*Hope (now played by Robin
Matson) became smitten
with artist Ben McFarren
(Stephen Yates), 1977.*

*Sara (still played by Millette
Alexander) found comfort
in the arms of Dr. Justin
Marler (Tom O'Rourke),
1977.*

him and threatened Spence with bigamy charges unless Spence produced Jimmy. Mike and Ann returned to Springfield and Ann began to help Mike out at the office to pay for her bills.

Leslie was somewhat uncomfortable with this arrangement, but soon realized that Ann was not out to steal her husband and Leslie and Ann became friends. Spence showed up in town and began to make drunken, abusive calls to Ann, threatening her to drop legal proceedings against him or she would never see Jimmy again. One night, Spence followed Ann to Mike's house, and in an alcoholic rage, punched Mike and knocked him out cold. Spence fled the scene in a panic, pulling out of the driveway so fast that he ran over Leslie, who had just arrived home. Ann called ambulances for both Mike and Leslie and they were rushed to Cedars.

Mike regained consciousness, but Leslie had severe injuries and needed surgery. After the operation, Leslie told Mike to tell Freddy that he would grow into a fine man like his father and uncle. She smiled weakly, told Mike that he had been a wonderful husband, and quietly died. Mike was devastated, but pulled himself together when he realized that Ann had gone after Spence. When Mike found the two, Spence was holding Ann at gunpoint! Mike was able to convince Spence that the authorities would be lenient on Spence since Leslie's death had been accidental. Spence cried that he couldn't live with the guilt anymore, threw down the gun, and told Ann where she could find Jimmy. After visiting Jimmy, Ann decided that he would be better off with Spence's relatives and returned to Springfield with Mike.

As Mike dealt with his wife's death, another Springfield resident also had to come to grips with the death of a spouse. Sara Werner's husband Joe had suffered a fatal heart attack shortly after he and Sara had adopted T.J., an abandoned ten-year-old boy who had been brought to Cedars. Sara found emotional support in Dr. Justin Marler, an old fiancé, who had been transferred from Chicago to Cedars. Justin was brash and opinionated, but he was gentle with Sara. Although Sara eventually stopped mourning Joe's death, she was unable to really respond to Justin's romantic overtures because of memories of Justin jilting her to marry the daughter of his wealthy supervisor.

When Justin's former supervisor, Emmet Scott, had heart trouble, he flew to Springfield to be treated by Justin. Emmet's spoiled daughter Jackie followed and flirted outrageously with her ex-husband, much to the annoyance of Justin and the dismay of Sara. More than one intimate moment between Sara and Justin was spoiled by a surprise visit from Jackie, who seemed more interested in causing trouble than winning Justin back. Although Justin assured Sara that his and Jackie's divorce had been too acrimonious to permit a reconciliation, Sara remained intimidated by this ghost from the past.

Also intimidated by her past was nurse Rita Stapleton. Texan Malcolm Granger arrived in town, and Rita seemed frantic in denying knowing who he was. It turned out that Rita had been the private nurse of Malcolm's elderly father, Cyrus, who had left Rita a sizable amount in his will and cut off Malcolm with nary a penny. Malcolm was in town to demand that Rita hand over her inheritance or face charges of murdering old Cyrus! When Malcolm ended up dead at Cedars, Malcolm's wife Georgene showed up and pointed the finger at Rita. Rita was arrested for murder and Mike Bauer rushed to her aid. Ed Bauer also backed Rita up and even proposed marriage once the trial was over.

The proposal only depressed Rita, who couldn't fully confide in either Bauer brother. The night old Cyrus had died, Rita had been with another Granger employee, who now lived in Springfield. His name was Roger Thorpe! Roger begged Rita to keep quiet about the past since another seedy revelation might well break up his marriage to Peggy. Rita agreed, knowing quite well how Ed resented Roger sleeping with Holly during Holly and Ed's marriage. When it

Ben married Eve Stapleton
(Janet Grey), 1978.

appeared that Rita was going to be found guilty, Roger stepped forward and told the jury that he was with Rita the night Cyrus died. Peggy was stunned and eventually divorced Roger. She and little Billy moved to Boise, Idaho.

Ed was so hurt by the revelation that he didn't even show up the day when the jury found Rita not guilty. Ed began seeing a lot of Holly again, and the two still pretended to the world that Christina was their child. But after months of intimacy, Holly realized that Ed still loved Rita and could more easily forgive Rita's mistakes than Holly's adultery. Rita and Ed began seeing each other again, and Holly stepped aside for a while, but began to have hope again when Ed and Rita never seemed to set the date for their marriage.

Rita's kid sister Eve also stalled about setting a wedding date. Eve had started seeing artist Ben McFarren, but was very cautious about the relationship, knowing that Ben still had feelings for his ex-fiancée Hope. Just when Eve started feeling really loved, Ben's brother Jerry came back into town and confessed to Hope that it was he, Jerry, who had robbed the deli the year before. Overhearing this and believing that Hope would not want Ben back, poor Eve tearfully ran down a garden path and fell on a stone stairway.

The injury led to blindness, and although Eve came to believe that Ben would never want Hope back after she refused to trust him, Eve still refused Ben's proposal. Eve felt that her blindness would only prove a burden to Ben. But Eve soon changed her mind. Rita was being harassed with phone calls by Georgene Granger, who had really murdered Cyrus and Malcolm. As the police were closing in on her, Georgene attempted a final revenge, setting fire to Rita's apartment. But it was blind Eve, instead, who was trapped in the blaze. Ben arrived to save her, and Eve agreed that she and Ben could have a wonderful life together. They married and Eve was later cured of her blindness.

It was a new era for Springfield when the powerful Spaulding Enterprises built its new headquarters there. Mike Bauer was hired as chief counsel for the corporation, and he soon became involved in the personal lives of the company president, the dynamic Alan Spaulding, and his sensual wife Elizabeth, who was dominated by Alan. When Elizabeth expressed an interest in renewing her photography career, Mike encouraged her, but Alan was very much opposed to the idea. Supposedly Alan feared that Elizabeth would neglect their school-age son Phillip, but Elizabeth began to suspect that Alan was envious of anything in her life that didn't revolve around him.

When Alan gave Phillip's governess, the shifty Diane Ballard, a new job as his personal secretary, it was the beginning of many nights of Alan and Diane "in conference." Elizabeth realized that Alan wanted her to be intimidated by the thought of competition, but Alan was totally unprepared when Elizabeth filed for divorce and custody of Phillip—with Mike agreeing to represent her. Although Mike had been seeing a lot of divorcée Jackie Marler, she was too free-spirited for him to get really serious about. Without looking for a woman who could fill the void in his life since Leslie's death, Mike had found her: she was his boss's wife, Elizabeth Spaulding!

About the same time, Mike was honored as the local Man of the Year. Although many people offered their congratulations, there was one man who wanted to tell Mike how proud he was. But he dared not see Mike or any of the other Bauers because they all thought he was dead. Bill Bauer *wasn't* killed in the Alaskan plane crash years before. In fact, he hadn't even gotten on the plane at all. Bill had run off with his girl friend Simone Kincaid and settled in Canada, where they had raised a daughter, Hillary. In Canada, Hillary noticed Bill's great interest in the Rita Stapleton trial and took a trip to Springfield to investigate.

Hillary found no clues for Bill's interest, but instead found an excellent nursing school, where she began her training. Hillary was taken ill with appendicitis and Bill secretly flew to Springfield to visit her. Once there, Bill was exposed, and Bert's shock at his reappearance grew to anger and resentment. Ed was so traumatized that he turned back to booze. Eventually Bill was forgiven by his Springfield family, but found that his staying on would cause pain to Bert, so he moved to Chicago. Hillary remained behind and soon became very close to her half brothers, Mike and Ed, as well as their mother Bert.

Mike quickly turned his attention to the divorce proceedings of Alan and Elizabeth Spaulding. Alan paid a Spanish nobleman, Ramon DeVillar, to sign a phony affidavit stating that he had been Elizabeth's lover for many years. Subsequently, Alan was awarded custody of Phillip. Elizabeth was devastated, but Mike vowed he would not rest until she got custody of Phillip. Mike also proposed marriage and Elizabeth accepted. Furious that Elizabeth would consider such an idea, Alan told Elizabeth that her dreams of marriage and children with Mike was a farce: she could never have children, and furthermore, Mike had known this for months! Stunned, Elizabeth broke off her engagement to Mike.

After Alan and Elizabeth's divorce, Jackie became chummy with Alan, but Jackie seemed really interested only in winning young Phillip's trust and affection—for good reason: Phillip was Jackie's natural son! One day, Jackie ran into a pushy reporter, Brandy Shellooe, and the encounter brought forth a flood of memories. Years before, while married to Justin Marler, a pregnant Jackie caught Justin in bed with Brandy Shellooe. Jackie ran off for Europe for a

After Leslie's death, Mike fell in love with Elizabeth Spaulding (Lezlie Dalton, right), but was shamelessly pursued by Jackie Marler (Cindy Pickett), 1978.

divorce and let Justin think that she had aborted their unborn child. Jackie actually had the baby and placed him for adoption in the hands of Dr. Paul LaCrosse.

Dr. LaCrosse was also Elizabeth's obstetrician, and when Elizabeth gave birth to a stillborn baby, Alan arranged that Jackie's baby be substituted. The "adoption" was hardly legal and when Elizabeth came to, the baby was presented to her as her own. Jackie had snooped in Dr. LaCrosse's office, so she knew exactly who had her son and kept tabs on him through the years. After Alan was awarded custody of Phillip, both Alan and Phillip became very fond of Jackie. It wasn't long before Alan proposed marriage. Alan knew that Jackie would hardly be the submissive, understanding wife Elizabeth had been, but he was intrigued by the idea of "taming" her. Although Jackie had many doubts about the marriage, she finally gave in, seeing this as her only opportunity to be a mother to Phillip.

After Elizabeth eventually forgave Mike Bauer for not telling her that she was unable to have children, they made plans to marry. Mike began also to investigate the lying Ramon DeVillar, who had swung the custody case in Alan's favor. When DeVillar began to waver, Mike went to see him, confident this liar would spill his guts. When Mike arrived he found DeVillar's guts spilled, all right: he had been shot to death! The killer turned out to be Dean Blackford, Alan's lawyer. Dean was married to Sara McIntyre. Sara and Dean had had a whirlwind courtship after Sara decided that she couldn't trust Justin Marler anymore. Slowly, Sara became aware of Dean's dirty dealings with Alan Spaulding and the couple often argued about it. Afraid that Sara would expose him, Dean tried to push Sara off a cliff, but Mike arrived in the nick of time and Dean fell to this death.

Although Mike was unable to prove Alan was behind the DeVillar murder or the purged testimony, Mike did open the custody case and Phillip was awarded to Elizabeth. This greatly displeased Phillip, who had grown fond of Jackie and believed Alan's continual badmouthing of Mike. Phillip came to hate Mike, and Elizabeth was furious that Alan could manipulate the boy so. When Phillip collapsed and was rushed to Cedars, Dr. Justin Marler performed heart surgery that saved the boy's life—completely unaware that he was operating on his own son! Elizabeth and Justin grew closer afterwards, and when Elizabeth broke off with Mike, Elizabeth married Justin. Thus Phillip's four "parents" had all married one another!

Meanwhile, Ben and Eve rented a cottage on the estate of wealthy, neurotic Lucille Wexler. Lucille would recall having been beaten by a former lover and would fantasize having a young stud at her beck and call. Lucille had a college-age daughter, Amanda, whom she dominated completely, constantly telling Amanda that men could not be trusted and that sex was filthy. Amanda tried to have a normal marriage to businessman Gordon Middleton, but Lucille's interference contributed to Amanda's frigidity and the end of the marriage. When Amanda returned under Lucille's wing, Lucille schemed to pair Amanda with the handsome Ben, who was exactly the boy/man material Lucille's fantasies were made of.

Ben encouraged Amanda to stand on her own two feet and Amanda attempted a reconciliation with Gordon, but to no avail. Ben was a loyal friend to Amanda through all of this, and Eve grew very jealous, spurred on by Lucille, who made Eve terribly insecure about all the women in Ben's life. Eve began nagging Ben about working overtime at his job at Spaulding Enterprises's Art Department. There Ben found a sympathetic shoulder on vixen Diane Ballard, and the fun-loving Diane seduced Ben. When Eve found out about the fling, she divorced Ben. Ben then turned to Amanda; they eventually slept together during a driving rainstorm. Still, Ben did not propose to Amanda, hoping for a reconciliation with Eve, the only woman he really wanted.

Eve's sister Rita was finally able to help Ed Bauer kick his drinking problem and his resentment of her, and Ed and Rita became engaged. Holly fantasized about breaking up the couple, but she had matured from her younger, manipulative days and put those dreams aside. Holly found herself being pursued by Roger once again. Holly didn't know that Roger had recently been diagnosed as sterile and how much Roger resented that Christina—who was to be Roger's only child—was the legal daughter of Ed Bauer. In fact, Roger became perversely competitive with Ed, and began an affair with Ed's sister Hillary, who mistook Roger's smooth line for utter devotion. Roger also flirted outrageously with Ed's fiancée Rita, who was disturbed by Roger's aggressive attentions.

One night, Roger forced his way into Rita's apartment, taunting her, asking her how long it would take until Rita would want to take him back to her bed.

Little Christina (Cheryl Lynn Brown) was about the only bright spot in the life of troubled Roger Thorpe (Michael Zaslow), 1979.

<u>October 11, 1978</u>

Roger's Rape of Rita

Roger: You've really held out on me. At the trial, I saved your pretty little neck.

Rita: I never said you didn't!

Roger: I gave you the alibi you needed, and it cost me everything! My home, my marriage . . . and for what? So you could turn on me and tell me I'm not a man?

Rita: Roger, if you touch me, I'll scream.

Roger: Scream. It'll do you more harm than good. Nobody's going to care about you. They'll figure: what you got, you asked for.

Rita: That's not true.

Roger: Cops are on to women like you. You're like . . . prostitutes who scream rape when they don't get paid.

Rita: (GETTING DESPERATE, TREMBLING WITH FEAR.) Roger, please . . . What do I have to do to get you to . . . just go?!

Roger: Pay up.

Rita: I can't.

Roger: You can try. You've got a lot to make up to me for. For gypping me out of money which was rightfully mine. For acting as if I don't exist. For putting me down to Hillary. And baby, for throwing Ed Bauer in my face. I've had just about all I can take of Dr. Ed from you or anyone else. Yeah, you owe me.

ROGER SUDDENLY WRAPS RITA'S ROBE AROUND HER LIKE A
STRAIGHTJACKET, SO SHE CAN'T MOVE, HOLDING HER BY IT.

Rita: Roger, let me go.

HE BEGINS TO RUN HIS HAND OVER HER ROBED BODY, TO RUN
HIS HAND THROUGH HER HAIR. BUT EVERY CARESS ENDS AS A
BLOW, A TUG, A YANK. HIS ANGER AND HATRED, AS WELL AS
HIS PASSION, ARE MOUNTING.

Rita: (STRUGGLING.) Roger, let me go.

Roger: (FURIOUS.) Shut up!

Rita: (STRUGGLING TO GET FREE.) You're a . . .
          coward . . . a weakling . . . You're not half
          the man Ed Bauer is. Trying to prove you're
          a man when you're not a man at all . . .

RITA TEARS HIS SHIRT AND SCRATCHES HIS BACK WITH HER
RING. WE WILL NEED THE SHOT OF THE SCRATCH WITH RING IN
A LATER SCRIPT. IT IS IMPORTANT TO GET A CLEAR SHOT OF
THIS.

Roger: Jesus . . . You scratched me. I don't like
          the way you've been behaving, Rita, baby.
          You've been treating me like a . . . non—
          person. Well, I'm not a non—person. I exist.
          I exist. Touch me. I'm real . . . Touch me.

RITA SLAPS ROGER, TRIES TO HIT HIM AGAIN.

Roger: Oh, you're going to play rough, are you? (HE
          STARTS FOR HER.) You owe me so much, Rita.

THE PHONE RINGS. WITH A TERRIBLE EFFORT, SHE SHOVES
HIM WITH HER FULL STRENGTH AND RACES FOR THE PHONE. HE
CATCHES UP WITH HER, GRABS HER BY THE SHOULDERS, AND
THROWS HER TO THE FLOOR.

```
    Rita:       (IMMOBILIZED, HER HAND TO HER HEAD, IN
                PAIN.) Oh . . .

    Roger:      You little bitch. You owe me. And I'm
                collecting . . .

    RITA, ON FLOOR, IS STRUGGLING TO SIT UP. HER SLIP IS
    PULLED UP, REVEALING BOTH THIGHS. ONE SHOULDER STRAP
    HAS FALLEN. SHE IS DAZED, TRYING TO ORIENT HERSELF.
    SHE BECOMES AWARE OF ROGER'S FEET AND LEGS. SHE LOOKS
    UP AND SEES ROGER STANDING OVER HER.

    Rita:       (TERRIFIED, SHE CAN ONLY HOLD UP ONE HAND
                WEAKLY TO FEND HIM OFF.) No . . . No . . .
```

Rita slapped him, and Roger hit back, forced her to the floor, and raped her. Rita, convinced no one would believe her, because of her past history with Roger, did not bring charges against him. Meanwhile, Roger went on his merry way, sleeping with the innocent Hillary while wooing Holly at the same time. When Roger told Hillary that he was going to marry Holly, Hillary felt cheap, sordid, but not as cheap as when he seduced her again after his marriage to Holly.

Rita did marry Ed, and they enjoyed a wonderful honeymoon in New York. But Holly was not happy with Roger, and refused to tell Christina that Roger was her natural father. Roger grew abusive with Holly, then raped her also. Holly filed charges of marital rape, and there was much public interest in the case. Alan wanted to fire Roger because of the bad publicity, but Roger knew all about Dean Blackford and the DeVillar affidavit, and threatened to expose Alan. Alan agreed to promote Roger to the vice presidency, the position Alan had promised Diane, and she became suspicious and investigated. Discovering Roger's hold over the boss she loved, Diane won Alan's gratitude, especially when Diane vowed to get the goods on Roger Thorpe.

Alan, unaware of how close Roger was to betraying him, brought in Ross Marler, Justin's younger brother, to act as Roger's attorney. Ross's tough examination of Holly made Roger appear innocent. Finally, Rita, when it looked like Roger would be acquitted, came forward at the last minute and testified that Roger had raped her also. No one was relieved when Roger was found guilty, for he was out on bond, and was threatening everyone. When Roger began beating Ed, Holly went to a drawer and picked out a gun. Reliving Roger's brutal rape of her, Holly emptied three bullets into Roger.

Holly was convicted of murder, but there was chicanery working behind the scenes: Roger had not actually died after the shooting, but had been whisked off to Alan Spaulding's private clinic in Puerto Rico. While Holly was in prison, Ed insisted on taking Christina into his home with Rita, but Rita soon found herself at odds with the little girl. Holly's mother Barbara, who was always comparing Rita unfavorably with Holly, insisted that Christina would be better off living with her.

Meanwhile, Jackie was not happy with Alan or her pregnancy, but she was so happy to be living with Phillip that she pushed her discontentment aside. But then Alan disappeared, his plane going down somewhere in the Caribbean. Alan and Hope (Alan's new employee and the daughter of Mike Bauer) swam to a deserted island. There they shed their hostility, inhibitions and clothes—

After Roger raped her, Holly filed charges against him, then shot him, 1979.

November 27, 1979

Under hypnosis, Holly tries to remember her shooting
of Roger, but the rape and shooting—two separate
incidents—come out as a single terrible nightmare.

Holly: I feel strange, like things are closing
                 in one me . . . Roger . . .

Dr. Quinn: Holly, you can see it clearly. Tell us
                 what happened.

Holly: (ABRUPTLY.) Roger said: "Lets get
                 something straight. I'm your husband, I
                 have rights here." (CUT TO ED'S SURPRISE
                 AND BEWILDERMENT. HOLLY IS SUPPOSED TO
                 BE DESCRIBING THE SHOOTING, NOT THE
                 RAPE. INTERCUT WITH BRIEF SILENT
                 FLASHBACKS FROM THE RAPE.) He said: "You
                 love him, don't you. I've seen the way
                 you look at him every time he comes over
                 to see Christina. Why don't you ever
                 look at me that way." I said: "I've
                 tried to love you—you wouldn't let me."
                 (ABRUPTLY, DESPERATELY.) I want to get
                 away. Please, Roger, I want to leave.
                 But he grabs me—he kisses me.

Dr. Quinn: (FIRMLY.) Holly, he didn't touch you.

Holly: *Yes*.

Dr. Quinn: Holly, Dr. Bauer was there, and he says
                 Roger didn't touch you.

Holly: He *did*—he did . . . Roger says Rita
                 asked for it. Ed hits him. Roger and Ed
                 are fighting.

CUT TO A MONTAGE OF THE SHOOTING AND THE RAPE. HOLLY IS
UNAWARE THAT THE JUMPS FROM ONE EVENT TO ANOTHER MAKE NO
SENSE. SHE RELIVES IT EMOTIONALLY AS IF IT HAPPENED THAT
WAY.

> I say "Roger, I *did* care for you—I
> wouldn't have married you *if I* didn't.
> He keeps coming at me. (ABRUPT JUMP.) He
> has a gun in his drawer—He says he could
> kill Ed and everyone'll think it was
> self-defense. (ABRUPT JUMP.) Roger
> keeps coming at me. I say no, no, no. He
> grabs me and tries to kiss me, but I push
> him away. His eyes—he's so angry.
> (ABRUPT JUMP.) Then Roger hits him, and
> Ed's lying on the floor. Roger hits him
> again—kicks him . . .

Dr. Quinn: And what do you do?

Holly: (REMEMBERING FOR THE FIRST TIME.) I go
               to get the gun.

Dr. Quinn: Where is it?

Holly: In the drawer of Roger's desk—I know
               it's there. I've never held a gun
               before—the metal's so smooth . . . cold
               . . .

Dr. Quinn: You picked up the gun?

Holly: Yes . . . and Roger says, "You shouldn't
               have come here, Bauer—you think you can
               fool with my wife, but I can't touch
               yours?" I point the gun at him. (ABRUPT
               JUMP.) I won't let him kiss me—I push
               him away—I'm afraid—his eyes, so full
               of hate. (ABRUPT JUMP.) He

```
                     goes to the desk for the gun to shoot Ed.
                     But I have the gun. He looks up and sees
                     me. He says, "What the hell are you
                     doing, Holly? It's still Ed, isn't it?
                     Still protecting Ed—you love him,
                     don't you—you love him, don't you?"
                     (ABRUPT JUMP.) He comes at me. He says,
                     "Holly, you're not going to turn me down
                     this time." My hand is shaking, but I
                     point the gun at him—I squeeze the
                     trigger. He stops—he's hit—I fire the
                     gun again—and again—three times. He
                     falls.

Dr. Quinn:           (FIRMLY.) Why did you fire the gun?

Holly:               (STILL IN TRANCE.) He was going to rape
                     me again. I couldn't bear it.
```

making wild passionate love on the beach. While they were missing, Jackie miscarried and was consoled by her former boyfriend, Mike Bauer. In fact, Mike and Jackie were thrown together fairly often during the search, never giving up hope that the two would be found.

Stranded, Alan talked openly to Hope about his tireless quest for success and how he regretted so many of his ruthless decisions along the way. Hope was touched by Alan's honesty, and her love for him grew. When Hope and Alan were found it became perfectly obvious what had gone on, and Jackie filed for divorce with the stipulation that she was welcome to visit Phillip anytime. Mike continued his custom of representing Alan's estranged wives, and did his damnedest to convince Hope that Alan was guilty of bribery, blackmail, and being an accessory to murder. But Hope saw Alan as a changed man and didn't consider any of Mike's charges well substantiated. Hope told Alan that if they had a long engagement, Mike would surely come around.

Mike's brother Ed and his wife Rita had put up with so much of Barbara Thorpe's interference in their raising Christina that Ed surprised Rita with a vacation in the Caribbean. Just as Rita felt her relationship with Ed was improving, an emergency phone call came from Springfield. Holly had been stabbed in the abdomen by a jealous inmate. Ed rushed home to wait out Holly's long operation, leaving Rita to enjoy the island. Rita took in the nightlife there and accidentally ran into an old flame from her hometown of Bluefield, Dr. Greg Fairbanks. Rita poured out her heart to Greg, then poured out of her dress. Imagine Rita's shock when she returned to Springfield to find herself pregnant. Unsure of who the father was, Rita was thrown into a quandry when Greg got a job at Cedars.

Rejected by Rita, Greg settled for the affections of Rita's younger sister, Eve. Ben, still hoping for a reconciliation with Eve, warned Eve about Greg's reputation, and Eve told Ben to mind his own business. But when Eve found that Greg was obsessed with Rita, Eve lashed out at Rita, telling her that she would never speak to her again. Then Eve realized that she still loved Ben and wanted him back. Eve burst into Ben's cabin and told him how much she regretted letting her pride get in the way of their happiness and that she loved him more than ever. At that moment Amanda came out of the bedroom in a nightgown. Ben explained that he and Amanda had been married that weekend. Eve apologized and ran out, humiliated.

Amanda's marriage to Ben did not thrill Lucille, Amanda's mother. Lucille realized Ben was too stubborn and independent to be the submissive son-in-law she craved. Lucille entered into a scheme with the ambitious Ross Marler to break up Amanda and Ben, then marry Amanda off to Ross, whose loyalty Lucille could depend upon. But then a secret emerged that sent Lucille into a panic. Everybody wanted to know why Alan Spaulding's ailing father Brandon asked to meet with Amanda in his nursing home. When Lucille heard of the visit, she rushed to confront old Brandon, who had been her lover many years before. Brandon urged Lucille to tell Amanda that she was his granddaughter. When Brandon suffered cardiac arrest during an argument, Lucille watched and waited until he was dead before sneaking out of the room.

Brandon Spaulding's will left all of Brandon's shares in Spaulding Enterprises to Amanda, but no one knew why. There were many theories tossed around as to Amanda's true paternity, but nothing seemed to pan out. At the same time Amanda was attempting to decipher the true facts of her parentage, the issue of young Phillip Spaulding's paternity also came to the fore. Phillip became quite confused when Alan left Jackie, whom he adored, to marry Hope. The divorced Jackie became reinterested in Mike Bauer, but Mike was still in love with Elizabeth. When Mike and Elizabeth found themselves together in Aspen, they had dinner and made love. Unfortunately, Jackie burst into Mike's

After his wife, Barbara, divorced him because of his son, Roger, Adam Thorpe (Robert Milli) eventually married Dr. Sara McIntyre.

room and discovered the lovers. Shattered, Jackie wondered whether to tell Justin about his wife Elizabeth's infidelity in Colorado.

One man who was never plagued by indecision was Roger Thorpe, obsessed with revenge against Ed, Holly, and Rita. Back in Springfield, Roger made plans to kidnap his daughter, Christina. He dressed up as a clown for a charity bazaar Cedars Hospital was sponsoring. Christina was amused by him, but just as she was to run into his arms, Holly and Ed called her over. As Roger cursed, Rita passed by. Hearing Roger's voice, Rita panicked and ran, and Roger followed her into a house of mirrors where he pulled a gun on her and dragged her away to a remote cabin to plot his next move.

The pregnant Rita was constantly on edge with Roger. But he did allow her to call the hospital to find out the results of her tests, which would tell her whether Ed or Greg was the father of her baby. When the tests proved Ed was the father, Roger was furious and kept Rita tied to a bed. When Roger heard

Roger kidnapped Holly and dragged her through the jungles of the Dominican Republic, 1980.

police radio broadcasts reporting that the cops were on their way to the cabin, he fled, ignoring Rita's screams that she was in labor. In his haste to flee, Roger knocked over a lantern, which set the cabin on fire. Mike and Ed rescued Rita and rushed her to Cedars, but not in time to save her baby's life. Both Ed and Mike vowed they wouldn't rest until Roger was brought to justice.

Unaware that Roger was bugging his phone, Ed flew Holly and Christina to Santo Domingo until Roger was caught. Waiting in the Dominican Republic was Roger, who tried to abduct Christina. While Holly distracted Roger, Christina escaped, and an outraged Roger dragged Holly miles through the jungle, with Mike and Ed in hot pursuit. Holly tried not to antagonize Roger, but they argued about Ed, and Roger told her that Ed had been cuckolded again: Rita had thought that Greg Fairbanks was the father of her baby. Finally, Mike and Ed caught up with Roger, and as Mike led Holly to safety, Roger shot Ed in the arm, then Roger almost fell off a cliff. As Ed struggled to pull the man who had

After her ordeal with Roger and with her marriage to Ed on the rocks, Rita struck up a torrid affair with wealthy industrialist Alan Spaulding (Christopher Bernau), 1981.

done so much harm to his family to safety, Roger lost his grip, and with a bloodcurdling scream, fell off the cliff to his presumed death.

With all of Springfield rocking from Roger's death, other secrets began unraveling. Jackie suffered a concussion and was treated at Cedars by her ex-husband Justin. While still unconscious, Jackie mumbled some phrases which made Justin realize that he was Phillip's father. About the same time, Elizabeth located Dr. LaCrosse, who confessed that, indeed, it was genetically impossible for Elizabeth to be Phillip's mother and that it was he, Dr. LaCrosse, who had substituted Phillip for Elizabeth's stillborn child. Shattered, Elizabeth remained in Europe where she came to the realization that her marriage to Justin was over. Soon, Jackie and Justin Marler, Phillip's natural parents, concluded that they belonged together and remarried.

After months of psychiatric therapy, Elizabeth returned to Springfield. Elizabeth decided that Phillip should live with Jackie and Justin, requesting

Alan to relinquish custody. Infuriated, Alan threatened to expose Elizabeth's affair in Aspen, but Hope overheard Alan's threats and was horrified. Hope insisted that Alan sign Phillip over to Jackie and Justin, which Alan did. But Alan resented Hope's interference and their marriage began crumbling. Alan soon found comfort in the arms of Rita Bauer, and Rita and Alan's affair continued even after Alan found that his wife Hope was pregnant.

When the affair was exposed, Ed had had enough of Rita and divorced her. Rita left town for parts unknown, not even telling Eve where she was headed. Hope was humiliated, but after she gave birth to a son, Alan Michael, she and Alan reconciled. But Alan soon became upset by a friend Hope made at Cedars Hospital. He was Andy Norris, who returned to Springfield after an absence of several years to write a biography of magnate Alan Spaulding. Andy began dating nurse Katie Parker, but he had ulterior motives. Andy knew Katie had the keys to psychiatrist Sara McIntyre's files. Andy raided the files and began blackmailing the town's most prominent citizens. The police were called in and eventually Andy was caught. Andy's mother turned for comfort to ex-husband Adam Thorpe, who had recently married Sara McIntyre and was only able to offer Barbara friendship. Needing a fresh start, Barbara moved to Switzerland to be with Holly and Christina.

January 4, 1980
Katie's New Year's Resolutions

Hillary: Katie, you're really painting yourself
into a corner. It's just your stupid New
Year's resolutions, and now you act as if
they're written in stone or something.
Stop playing hard to get. Go with Mark to
the party.

Katie: (WEAKENING, BUT STILL RESISTING.)
Hillary, it's a matter of *character*.

Hillary: It's *unnatural*—and you're also twisting
             yourself into a pretzel being nice to your
             brother—you know you don't *want* to . . .
             And acting so indifferent to Mark—it's
             absolutely crazy! Look, it's already the
             fourth. You've kept your two resolutions
             for four days—that's better than last
             year. Now *drop* it.

FLOYD ENTERS AND APPROACHES THE NURSES DESK.

Floyd: (AMIABLY) Hi, Sis. Hi, Hillary.

Hillary: Hi, Floyd.

Floyd: Working late tonight, I see.

Hillary: Yep. You too, I see.

TAKE REACTION OF KATIE, UNREASONABLY ANNOYED.

Floyd: Yeah—they're keeping me busy. Hi again,
             Sis.

Katie: (WITH EFFORT.) Hi, Floyd.

Floyd: Yeah, I've got my hands full. I've kinda
             become the big gun of the maintenance
             crew, if I say so myself.

TAKE KATIE, FIGHTING AN IMPULSE TO LET HIM HAVE IT.

Hillary: (AMIABLY WRY.) The big gun, huh?

Floyd: Yeah . . . (PAUSE.) I could sure use a beer
             and a coupla tacos. That ''wholesome''
             food they push in the cafeteria really
             gets to me, you know. (KATIE IS A STEAM
             KETTLE ABOUT TO BLOW.) Know what I had for
             lunch? *Whole wheat* bread. (INCREDULOUS.)

| | Covered with those alfalfa sprouts—can you believe it? 'Looked like a little green bird's nest. Then little pieces of avocado. A hard-boiled egg—little pieces of bacon bits, but it's not really bacon—you ready for this? It's made outta *soy bean-flavored* like bacon. It was really disgusting. So I went up to the, uh, dietician, and I said, ''Hey, don't you at least have some ketchup to put on this mess?'' |

Katie: (THE KETTLE EXPLODES.) What's the matter with you? You think people want to hear you describe everything you had for lunch in gory detail? (FLOYD IS STUNNED, ESPECIALLY AFTER KATIE'S RECENT MILDNESS.) And why don't you comb your hair. You look like you just got out of bed—you *always* look like you just got out of bed! You're gonna have to straighten up one of these days, kiddo. You look like something the cat dragged in. You're *uncouth*. Nobody wants to get *near* you. Hillary won't go out with you, and who can blame her?—*nobody* will!

HILLARY SIGNALS SILENTLY TO FLOYD THAT KATIE IS NOT HERSELF.

Floyd: Hey, how come you've been so nice to me, and now all of a sudden it's back to normal? (HIDING HURT FEELINGS.) Well, nice talking to you, Hillary. I gotta get back to work. (FLOYD EXITS.)

Hillary: (HILLARY WATCHES KATIE FOR A MOMENT.) Well, you've broken *one* resolution. Now how about going for two?

Near the Spaulding estate, Lucille Wexler hired a Canadian woman, Jennifer Richards, as her live-in housekeeper. Driving into town, Jennifer and her husband Walter argued, and their car collided with Mike Bauer's car. Jennifer's husband was killed and Jennifer and her daughter, Morgan, were injured. Jennifer assured Mike that he was not the cause of the accident, but teenager Morgan accused Mike of killing her father. However, Morgan eventually apologized.

To catch up on her schoolwork, Morgan was being tutored by Kelly Nelson, Ed Bauer's idealistic godson, who had moved to Springfield to study medicine. Morgan and Kelly thought each other stuck up, but cooled their hostilities when their mutual friend, Tim (T.J.) Werner interceded. Kelly was dating Ed's sister Hillary, who had been very cautious around men ever since her experience with Roger Thorpe. Kelly also met Nola Reardon, the youngest of boarding house operator Bea Reardon's seven children. Nola dreamed of a life as glamorous and exciting as the old movies she adored.

Nola immediately became interested in Kelly. Here was husband material:

Pucker up: Floyd (Tom Nielsen) fell for Nola (Lisa Brown) hook, line, and sinker, 1980. (Al Rosenberg/ Sterling's Magazines.)

Kelly was kind, ruggedly handsome with a body that wouldn't quit; and as a doctor, he would surely bring Nola the wealth and prestige she deserved after years of slaving away at her mother's boarding house. Nola saw Hillary as competition at first, but then realized that there was a deep attraction between Morgan and Kelly, which neither seemed willing to admit. Nola sidled up to Morgan and began drawing up a master plan to hook her prize catch.

Meanwhile, Morgan was experiencing emotions for Kelly she did not understand. One day, she went to Laurel Falls to go swimming and met Kelly. Amidst the scenic summer beauty, Kelly was so enraptured by Morgan's innocent, tomboyish charm that he took her in his arms and made love to her. Afterwards, Morgan flipped out: she obviously wasn't prepared emotionally for a sexual relationship. Kelly also felt pangs of guilt for making love to such an impressionable young woman. Both Kelly and Morgan confided in Nola, who viciously told Morgan that Kelly had the entire hospital cafeteria in stitches telling them about the silly high school girl who had tried to make love to him like a woman.

Nola's machinations didn't work. Kelly Nelson (John Wesley Shipp) married Morgan Richards (Kristen Vigard), 1981.

Between Nola's lies and Morgan's guilt over her ostensible boyfriend Tim Werner, Morgan was so confused that she decided to run away, hiding in the back of Ben McFarren's van as he drove to Chicago. Ben had gone out of town to meet with art dealer Carter Bowden—Alex's son by his first marriage—to discuss Ben's artwork. So imagine Ben's surprise when he was arrested for transporting a minor across state lines. Eve, in Chicago visiting friends, bailed Ben out, and they became friends, deciding to put the past behind them. Ben had recently separated from Amanda after wealthy, spoiled Spaulding executive Vanessa Chamberlain told Ben that Amanda was secretly underwriting a major art show for him. A proud Ben told Amanda that she could not buy success for him, and since she obviously didn't think he had the talent to make it on his own, he wanted some time apart.

Amanda took the news bravely and didn't tell Ben that she was carrying his child. She moved back with Lucille and began confiding to Jennifer Richards, the housekeeper. In time, the sympathetic Jennifer became like a second mother to Amanda, and there was good reason for this: Jennifer was Amanda's natural mother! At age sixteen, Jennifer, whose real name was Jane Marie Stafford, had been seduced by Alan Spaulding. Jennifer's parents gave the baby girl to Brandon Spaulding, who entrusted Amanda's care to his former mistress Lucille Wexler. Now, years later, Jennifer had insinuated herself into Amanda's life, knowing full well that Lucille had raised Amanda as Lucille's own.

Jennifer had no intention of telling Amanda that she was her natural mother, but Lucille disbelieved her, having recently discovered Jennifer was the same Jane Marie Stafford who had given birth to Amanda. Lucille attacked Jennifer with a letter opener, screaming that she would kill before she would let anyone take Amanda away from her. Jennifer, trying to defend herself, pushed Lucille away and Lucille fell on the letter opener and died. Ben and Amanda walked in and discovered Lucille's body. Subsequently, Jennifer was arrested for murder.

Ross Marler, the assitant district attorney, vigorously prosecuted Jennifer, both to further his career and to win the gratitude of Amanda, who he hoped to marry. Since Jennifer would not admit why Lucille would even consider attacking her with a letter opener, Jennifer appeared guilty of manslaughter, and Ross won a conviction. However, Alan Spaulding recognized Jennifer as Jane Marie Stafford and the pieces began falling into place. Amanda, filled with remorse for having hated the mother who had only wanted to protect her, collapsed and miscarried. Ben vowed to stand by Amanda, but Amanda, fearing that Ben only was honor bound, pushed him aside, telling him she no longer needed him.

Meanwhile, Amanda's half sister Morgan seem to find herself in nothing but trouble. After running off to Chicago, she got involved with a teenage prostitution ring, and was saved by Kelly and Tim just before she would have to turn a trick. Once home, Nola's lies about Kelly intensified and Morgan turned to boyfriend Tim for comfort. But Tim was having his own problems with alcohol, and Morgan felt it necessary to stand by Tim until the young man got the help he needed. Kelly grew impatient for Morgan to admit her love for him and, dejected, he turned to Nola for sexual consolation.

When Morgan was kidnapped by the head of the Chicago prostitution ring, Duke Lafferty, who had broken out of jail, Kelly helped rescue her and Morgan was finally able to return Kelly's love. But Morgan made the mistake of confiding to the devious Nola her plan to break up with Tim. Nola got Tim drunk that evening, hoping that Morgan would feel sorry for Tim and delay breaking up with him. Morgan got into a car with Tim and they were involved in a serious accident, which resulted in Morgan requiring hours of surgery. Realizing the seriousness of his drinking problem, Tim was helped by recovering alcoholic Ed Bauer, who got Tim into A.A. to deal with his problem.

After Morgan's recovery, she and Kelly became engaged, and Nola grew frantic. Nola had not become pregnant with Kelly's child as planned, so she seduced Katie's brother Floyd Parker, a happy-go-lucky hospital handyman who was desperately in love with her. Nola became pregnant and tried to pass the baby off as Kelly's, claiming the baby was conceived in one night of lusty lovemaking when an inebriated Kelly had come to Nola. Kelly had actually passed out before anything happened but couldn't remember any of the details. Kelly offered to marry Nola and would have, if Bea Reardon hadn't stepped forward. Bea told Kelly that he had indeed passed out at the Reardons and Bea had made sure that Nola didn't bother him.

Enraged, Kelly confronted Nola, and Nola's months of deviousness were exposed. Soon afterwards, Kelly and Morgan were married in an outdoor ceremony at Laurel Falls, with a youth choir performing the couple's favorite song, "You Needed Me." That same day, Nola was scheduled to marry Floyd, who was willing to forgive her for past misdeeds, feeling that Nola would change with his love and support. But the "selfish" Nola surprised everyone with her mature decision not to marry Floyd, knowing that she didn't love him. Furthermore, Nola also refused financial assistance from Floyd during her pregnancy, telling him she would find a job to support herself.

When Vanessa Chamberlain—rich, impetuous, and beautiful—strolled into town, all of Springfield took notice. Vanessa was the daughter of the ever doting Henry Chamberlain, who had merged his business with the Spauldings.

<u>July 27, 1981</u>

Kelly: Nola, how far along are you really? Not
          three months, not long enough to have crying
          jags at the hospital and certainly not
          enough to be experiencing morning sickness.

Nola: You know, Kelly, you know why I told you
          that. You know I couldn't tell you about the
          pregnancy right away because I was afraid.

Kelly: You were afraid that I would find out the
          truth! That you were lying through your
          teeth! Oh, well that shouldn't have
          concerned you, when it comes to deception
          you are a real pro! You are the fastest damn
          liar I've ever known! But I have to give you
          credit. I have to give you absolute credit.
          You almost pulled it off, you really did,
          but then again, you were really working with
          a real patsy. I mean, I have this basic flaw
          in my character, I trust the people that I
          like, and you knew that, didn't you? So it
          looks like I made two big mistakes here. My
          first big mistake was to like you, and my
          second big mistake was to let you know it.

Nola: (TEARS STREAMING.) The reason, the reason
          you're saying all these things to me, the
          reason is because you feel guilty about the
          time we made love.

Kelly: We did *not* make love. Whatever, whatever the
          hell you want to call it, that baby is not
          mine. And don't play the victim, Nola,
          because it's not going to work. Morgan and I
          were almost the victims of your lies and
          tricks. Oh, I feel sorry for you. God I feel
          sorry for you.

Nola: (ANGER THROUGH HER TEARS.) I don't want your
          sympathy! I don't want your pity!

Kelly: You don't?

Nola: No!

Kelly: Well, I think it's pretty damn generous of me to be able to feel pity for someone who almost ruined my life and my chance for happiness with Morgan.

Nola: (A CRY AS SHE COVERS HER EARS.) Oh—I—hate—that—name!

Kelly: Well, how 'bout that? Think of all the time and energy you wasted trying to convince her you were her best friend. You know, Nola, you haven't felt an honest feeling for anybody.

Nola: For you! The feelings for you are all honest.

Kelly: That is the sickest lie of them all.

Nola: Everything I did was because I loved you, because I loved you and because I wanted to prove that I could make you happy.

Kelly: Including ruining my life? And my chances to be happy with Morgan.

Nola: Well, Kelly, why don't you just go back to her? Yeah, why don't you just go to her and see if she can make you happy.

Kelly: That's just what I'm gonna do. And I'll tell you what's next, Nola. I'm going to get down on my knees and I'm going to beg her forgiveness if I have to, for ever getting involved with you.

Kelly and Morgan (now played by Jennifer Cook) later honeymooned on the island paradise of Tenerife, 1981.

Years before, Vanessa had been engaged to the struggling Ross Marler, but jilted him in favor of a blueblooded fop who was in a perfect position to bail out Henry's failing company. Now free of this hasty marriage, Vanessa resolved to sink her hooks into Ross once again.

But Ross had matured from his ambitious, expedient early days and rejected Vanessa's advances, even when she showed up on his doorstep wearing nothing but a fur coat and high heels! Vanessa faked a suicide attempt to get Ross's attention, but it didn't work. However, Vanessa did attract Dr. Ed Bauer's best bedside manner and the two, to everybody's surprise, began to date. But when Ed's mind began to wander, Vanessa's coat-and-heels trick brought him back to earth. Ed eventually married Maureen Reardon, Nola's even-tempered older sister. Ross, on the other hand, continued to see Amanda Spaulding, who was still having severe emotional problems after her miscarriage and her mother's trial.

With the encouragement of Carrie Todd, a graphics artist at Spaulding Enterprises, Ross came clean with Amanda, confessing that he had once schemed with Lucille to come between Amanda and Ben. Completely shattered, Amanda retreated into fantasy, wearing little-girl dresses and playing the piano all day. But with therapy, Amanda snapped out of it, and her newly discovered father, Alan Spaulding, gave her a prestigious position at Spaulding. Carrie Todd helped Ross through the rough times afterwards, introducing him to jogging, health foods, and spiritual well-being. Ross fell madly in love with her, completely unaware that this epitome of clean living had a tragic past and that Carrie was hiding a terrible secret.

Suddenly, Springfield was rocked by two murders! The first was the death of Diane Ballard, the longtime, unrequited lover of Alan Spaulding. Alan seemed a likely suspect, especially after Diane realized that Alan would never leave his child bride, Hope. Diane began blackmailing Alan with tape recordings that proved Alan had obstructed the search for convicted rapist Roger Thorpe. But there were other suspects, too. The happily married Jackie and Justin Marler

It couldn't have happened to nicer folks: the murder victims, Diane Ballard (Sofia Landon) and Joe Bradley (Michael J. Stark), 1981.

were blackmailed by Diane, who threatened to tell Phillip that Jackie and Justin were Phillip's natural parents. Diane also had many unpleasant run-ins with Carrie Todd, but it was unclear why the two hated each other so. After Diane was found dead, suspicion focused on Diane's shifty sidekick, private eye Joe Bradley, but soon Joe was found dead and all of Springfield was in an uproar.

Panicking, Alan took Hope on a secret vacation to get away from the fracas. Certain that Alan was fleeing to avoid arrest, Mike finally tracked Alan down. Alan was arrested for obstruction of justice in the Roger Thorpe case and served several months in jail. Ross Marler joined Mike in the investigation into the slayings of Diane and Joe, and Ross was stunned when the real killer turned up right under his nose. The killer was Ross's girl friend Carrie Todd! On the witness stand, Carrie told of her marriage to Todd MacKenzie, who had committed suicide when he was framed on an embezzlement scheme orchestrated by Diane Ballard. The night of Diane's death, Diane had taunted Carrie about the past, and Carrie lost control and pushed Diane into a fireplace, where Diane hit her head and died. Later, Joe Bradley had pulled a gun on Carrie, and Carrie, acting in self-defense, had killed Joe. With other details falling into place, Carrie was found not guilty and Carrie and Ross quickly married.

While Alan was in prison, Amanda adapted to her role as president of Spaulding Enterprises with unusual aplomb. She was helped by Mark Evans, a new executive at the company, and the two began dating. Vanessa Chamberlain, who certainly made the rounds, tried to come between Amanda and Mark, but Amanda and Mark eventually broke up over Amanda's inability to participate in sexual relations. Mark left for vacation in Europe, where he looked up Amanda's mother Jennifer, who was on business for Spaulding. When Mark and Jennifer returned to Springfield married, Amanda was wracked with guilt about her feelings for her mother's husband. Mark told many conflicting stories about his past and continued to toy with the affections of both mother and daughter for months.

Vanessa, letting no grass grow under her feet, spotted new prey: Tony Reardon, the street-wise, handsome brother of Nola. Tony had fallen in love with Hillary Bauer, but when it seemed that Hillary was still torn between Kelly Nelson and lawyer Derek Colby, Tony had a wild weekend in Chicago with Vanessa. Tony realized his mistake and tried to cool it with Vanessa. Undaunted, Vanessa pulled out all the stops when she showed up at the Reardon boarding house in nothing but her coat and heels. The kindly Mrs. Bea Reardon asked Vanessa if she wasn't warm in that coat, and perhaps Bea could hang it up for her? Vanessa demurred and skeddadled. Later, she wrote Derek Colby an anonymous letter stating that Tony and Hillary spent the night together.

To escape reality, Nola
would often fantasize being
in one of her favorite
movies with Quinton
(Michael Tylo) as her co-
star. This time around she's
in Charlotte Brontë territory
as Springfield's Jane Eyre
crashes in the arms of her
Rochester, 1982.

Enraged, Tony assumed his snoopy sister Nola had penned the letter, since Nola had a history of butting into everybody's life. Tony confronted Nola with dire consequences. It was quite ironic that Nola, after years of manipulation, was now being wrongly accused of devious behavior. Nola had taken a job as a live-in assistant to the mysterious archeologist Quinton R. McCord, who lived in a remote mansion on the ominous-sounding Thornway Road. She managed to win Quinton's respect but couldn't bring herself to tell Quinton, who assumed Kelly was the father of Nola's baby Kelly Louise, that it was Floyd who was the real father. When Tony blew up at Nola, he revealed all of Nola's past devious-ness to Quinton and Floyd.

Nola's world fell apart. When Floyd threatened to sue for custody of Kelly Louise, Nola ran off with the baby, but returned to face the music. Later, she was kidnapped by the notorious Silas Crocker, who was the prime suspect in the unsolved London murder of one of Quinton's co-workers. After she was rescued by Quinton and Tony, Nola resumed her duties at the Thornway Road mansion.

Meanwhile, after her marriage to Ross Marler, Carrie suffered psychological problems and developed a multiple-personality disorder. When her second personality emerged, it wreaked havoc for all of Springfield. Carrie II was a selfish slut, who flirted outrageously with Alan Spaulding and caused the breakup of Jackie and Justin Marler's marriage by telling Ross and Jackie that Justin tried to rape her! Carrie II also made it very clear to Amanda, Eve, and the usually unflappable Vanessa to keep their grubby paws off Ross! The topper was Carrie II's sordid affair with Spaulding employee Josh Lewis, a spoiled rich kid from an Oklahoma oil family. When Ross discovered the two in bed, he walked out on her.

However, Dr. Sara McIntyre suspected correctly that Carrie suffered from a multiple-personality disorder and had Carrie committed for therapy. But Carrie II broke out of the hospital and snuck into Ross's bedroom intending to shoot him. However, the two personalities began fighting for control and Carrie I finally won out and threw the gun to the floor. Afterwards, Carrie elected to go to England for special treatment, but not before trying to undo the damage

There were few happy moments for the tortured Carrie (Jane Elliot) and her husband, Ross (Jerry verDorn), 1982.

Carrie II had done. She called Jackie and told her that Carrie II had lied about Justin attempting to rape her. Jackie rushed home to be reunited with Justin, but her plane crashed and she was presumed dead. Later, in England, Carrie divorced Ross, wanting Ross to find a life he deserved.

Another victim of the Carrie's fallout was Josh Lewis. He had become friendly with Morgan Nelson and admitted how guilty he was about the affair. Morgan encouraged Josh to apologize to Ross, which he did. Kelly, seeing the relationship between Josh and his wife blossom, was threatened by it, and they argued constantly about Josh. Kelly went along with Morgan to the Caribbean where she had a job modeling. Josh arrived unexpectedly, pretending to have business in the islands. He took Morgan for a boat ride, and the two had to spend the night together on a remote island when a serious storm broke out. Kelly was furious, punched Josh out, and separated from Morgan. Eventually, Morgan had a sexual relationship with Josh, but they agreed that marriage would be a mistake. Morgan left town to pursue a modeling career in New York.

After Carrie divorced him, Ross renewed his relationship with Amanda Spaulding, but Amanda was still torn with lust for her mother's husband Mark. In Spain on business, Mark and Amanda declared their love for each other, while attempting to rescue offshore oil workers stranded during a violent storm. Amanda planned to tell her mother all about the affair, but when Jennifer announced that she was pregnant, Amanda backed off. When Jennifer discovered the affair, she attacked both Mark and Amanda, then left town. At Spaulding Enterprises, Amanda was handed another disappointment as she was disposed of as president by her father Alan. Afterwards, Amanda, Ross, and Josh formed their own company, Los Tres Amigos (The Three Friends). Assisting Alan in the takeover was old Henry Chamberlain. Henry had spent years trying to find his illegitimate son and had finally located him in Springfield. Henry's son was none other than Quinton McCord! After many misunderstandings, Henry was finally reunited with his son.

However, Quinton was involved in his own domestic mess: for many years he had been taking care of a mysterious woman who lived on the third floor of his mansion. She was Mona Enright, who had allowed Quinton to believe that he had pushed her off a ledge, causing severe damage to her face and voice. Out of guilt, Quinton had seen Mona through years of reconstructive surgery and therapy. Little did Quinton know that when he pushed Mona years before, she had fallen only a few feet. It was then that Mona's lover, Samuel Pasquin, deliberately pushed her off the cliff.

When Mona discovered that Samuel Pasquin was living under an assumed name, she plotted her revenge. And Samuel Pasquin turned out to be none

They're off to see the Wizard: after the Mona Enright incident, Quinton (Michael Tylo) married Nola Reardon (Lisa Brown), 1983. Nola took a fire truck to the wedding, and the newlyweds took off for their honeymoon in a helium balloon.

other than Mark Evans! Mona lured Mark, Amanda, and Quinton to a cliff where she confronted Mark and told him that he must get rid of the woman he loved. As Mona tried to push Amanda off the cliff, Mark rushed to her defense and was shot by Mona. In the ensuing struggle, Mona fell to her death. Before dying, Mark told Amanda that although he had lied about many things, he never lied about loving her. Amanda was once again comforted by Ross Marler, but decided to leave town when her mother wrote asking for a reconciliation.

Before she left, Amanda sold her oil stock to the Lewis family, who began a new era in Springfield history. The Lewises consisted of patriarch H.B. (Harlan Billy), his daughter Trish, his sons Josh and Billy, and Billy's spoiled teenage daughter Mindy. To get the attention of Phillip Spaulding, Mindy accidentally-on-purpose got hurt in the horse stables and was rushed to the hospital. Mindy's roommate there was Beth Raines, a withdrawn young artist who soon attracted the attentions of both Rick Bauer and Phillip. Shy Beth went to the high school prom with Rick and was shocked when she was elected prom queen. But that was not all: Phillip, the catch of Springfield, confessed that he had fallen in love with her!

Her head spinning, Beth soon came back down to earth when her step-father was violently opposed to Beth seeing Phillip. Bradley Raines was a tough working-class man with a chip on his shoulder against those who are to the manor born. He was also a sick man, whose beating of Beth had brought her to the hospital. When Bradley was unsuccessful in his threats against Phillip, Bradley dropped a little bombshell that had Phillip's world falling apart: Phillip was a bastard and Alan Spaulding wasn't his father—Justin Marler was. Bradley next began beating up Beth, and when she fought back, Bradley raped her.

Beth went into a semi-catatonic state afterwards, and refused to tell anyone the full extent of Bradley's brutality. But she was able to pull herself together

The Class of 1983: mischievous Mindy Lewis (Krista Tesreau), self-destructive Phillip Spaulding (Grant Aleksander), prom Queen Beth Raines (Judi Evans), and good guy Rick Bauer (Michael O'Leary).

Guiding Light Milestones

The Eighties

1980.   On April Fool's Day, Roger is killed in the Dominican Republic.
In April, Ben McFarren marries Amanda.
In May, Hope Bauer and Alan Spaulding are wed.
In October, Lucille Wexler is killed during a struggle with
Jennifer Richards.

1981.   In January, Jennifer is vindicated in the Lucille Wexler case.
In March, Adam Thorpe and Sara McIntyre are wed.
In August, Kelly Nelson and Morgan Richards finally marry.
In September, Hope gives birth to Alan Michael.
In October, Diane Ballard and Joe Bradley meet their maker.

1982.   In January, Nola gives birth to Kelly Louise.
In March, Carrie Todd and Ross Marler are wed.
In June, Jennifer Richards and Mark Evans elope.
In July, Jackie Marler is presumed dead in a plane crash.

1983.   In February, Ed Bauer and Maureen Reardon tie the knot.
In May, the demented Mona Enright shoots and kills Mark Evans,
then leaps to her death.
In June, Nola Reardon is married to Quinton Chamberlain.
In August, Eli Sims murders Bill Bauer in Chicago.
In November, H.B. Lewis shoots and kills Eli Sims.

1984.   In February, Vanessa Chamberlain and Billy Lewis are wed.
In March, Phillip Spaulding and Mindy Lewis, as well as Warren
Andrews and Lesley Ann Monroe, are married.
In May, Annabelle Sims and Tony Reardon are wed.
In May, Lesley Ann dies.
In May, Nola Chamberlain gives birth to Anthony James.
In May, H.B. Lewis and Reva Shayne Lewis marry.
In September, Hillary Bauer is killed.

In November, Miss Piper gets her just desserts.

In December, India von Halkein blackmails Phillip Spaulding into marriage.

1985.   On Valentine's Day, Floyd Parker murders Andy Ferris.

In October, Clarie Ramsey gives birth to Michelle.

In November, Kurt Corday marries Mindy Lewis.

In November, H.B. Lewis III is born.

In December, Lujack dies.

In December, Maeve Stoddard and Kyle Sampson are wed.

1986.   In March, Bert Bauer passes away.

In May, Cain Harris is shot and killed by Kyle Sampson.

In May, Ben is born to Maeve.

---

enough to move out of her house and into the Reardon's boarding house. When Bradley showed up at Beth's college classroom with a court order for her to move back home, Phillip grabbed Beth and they ran off to New York, living in a prop storage area under Central Park. Rick and Mindy soon followed to warn the young lovers that Bradley was on their tail. At first, the spoiled Mindy wanted to reestablish her claim on Phillip, but once in the Big Apple, she found herself falling for Rick. Mindy, for whom "work" was an obscene word, even found that slinging hash could be rewarding!

Bradley finally tracked Beth and Phillip down, and tried to push Phillip off a cliff. Instead, Bradley slipped and was rescued by Beth. Although he promised to stay away from the two, Bradley soon began threatening Beth again. Beth filed charges against Bradley, and on the witness stand Bradley confessed all his past misdeeds. He was sent to prison, where he received the psychiatric help he needed.

On the day of Beth and Phillip's wedding, Mindy let it slip that she was pregnant with Phillip's child. Mindy's hot-headed father Billy confronted Mindy right in front of Beth, and Beth called a halt to the ceremony. At first Mindy considered letting Beth and Phillip adopt her baby, but she abruptly changed her mind, dumped Rick, and demanded that Phillip marry her. After a long talk with Billy, who told Phillip about his own very happy "shotgun" marriage, Phillip decided to marry Mindy. However, the newlyweds were soon at each other's throats, and Mindy lost the baby. Afterwards, the once close four friends were wary of any future alliances with one another.

Meanwhile, the teenagers' college English professor, Annabelle Sims, was attempting to deal with a past that threatened her sanity. Just before meeting Annabelle, Tony had found an old camera belonging to his father, who had mysteriously disappeared twenty years before. Developing the film, Tony found a photo of his father with a beautiful woman and four familiar faces—Brandon Spaulding, Henry Chamberlain, H.B. Lewis, and Bill Bauer. Annabelle Sims looked exactly like the young woman in the picture, but that seemed impossible since the photo was over twenty years old. Tony's sister Nola became interested in the photo and arranged to go to Chicago to talk with Bill Bauer about it. But before Nola got to Bill, he fell to his death from his hotel room window.

The police ruled the death accidental since there was a large amount of

After running away to New York, Beth and Phillip were befriended by a savvy Santa named Nick (Rex Everhart).

alcohol found in Bill's system. But Mike and Ed Bauer had their doubts: their father hadn't had a drop to drink in years—why now? When Henry Chamberlain saw Annabelle for the first time at a party, he collapsed with a heart attack and was in critical condition for weeks. When Henry recovered, he denied knowing anything about Annabelle or the photograph. Then H.B. Lewis was shot outside his apartment, but this tough old bird pulled through, and the culprit was revealed. It was Eli Sims, Annabelle's father, who was on a vendetta after the men who had toyed with the affections of his wife.

Eli took Annabelle to the exact site of Annabelle's mother's death, and suddenly Annabelle realized that as a child she had witnessed her mother's killing. The insane Eli had killed her mother, and now was trying to murder Annabelle (who was the spitting image of her mother) and Tony Reardon. Eli was stopped, however, when H.B. Lewis shot Eli dead with a high-powered rifle.

In 1983, Harley Kozak and Gregory Beecroft had dual roles as Annabelle and Tony Reardon (right photo) and as Annabelle's mother and Tony's father, Tom (left photo), in flashback scenes.

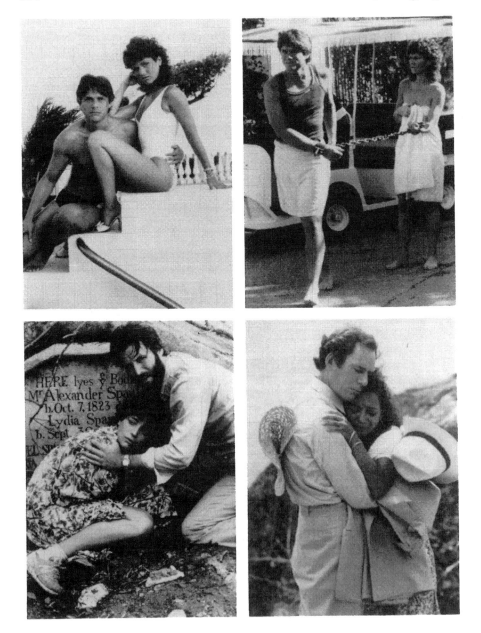

Although traumatized, Annabelle was able to take Tony to the place where her father had buried Tom Reardon two decades before. Tom had not deserted his family as thought, but had been murdered by the sick Eli. Tony married Annabelle and they moved into a turn-of-the-century cottage.

While Tony's fortunes were looking up, his friend Floyd's were not. Floyd had fallen in love with Lesley Ann Monroe, who had been a prostitute briefly, but had reformed and wanted to be a faithful wife to Floyd and a loving step-mother to Stacy. (Nola had changed her daughter's name from Kelly Louise to one of her favorite movie heroines, Anastasia—Stacy, for short.) But then, Lesley Ann met the new hospital administrator Warren Andrews, a ruthless, sophisticated older man, and was swept off her feet. She started seeing Warren on the side until Floyd found out and dropped her like a hot potato. Then everybody at Cedars Hospital was shocked when confirmed bachelor Warren married Lesley Ann in the most sparsely attended Springfield wedding in decades.

Shortly after the wedding, Lesley Ann was bitten by a mouse that had escaped from a Cedars Hospital lab. Lesley Ann came down with a rare tropical disease, which, freely translated, was called the Dreaming Death. Although doctors worked frantically to save her, Lesley Ann died, but not before wishing her old love Floyd every happiness. Two of the doctors working on her case, Jim Reardon and Claire Ramsey, soon became personally involved. Jim, Nola's other older brother, was a dedicated young researcher who had fallen in love

Investigating the Brandon Spaulding mystery in Barbados, reporter Fletcher Reade (Charles Jay Hammer) and Dr. Claire Ramsey (Susan Pratt) fought romantic feelings for each other (top, left), 1984. Although the notorious Miss Piper handcuffed them and left them for dead, Fletcher and Claire escaped with their lives but not with their clothes (top, right). Meanwhile, Annabelle Reardon (Harley Kozak) and her brother-in-law Dr. Jim Reardon (Michael Woods) hid from Miss Piper in an old graveyard (bottom, left). It turned out that Brandon Spaulding (Keith Charles) had years before fallen in love with a black woman, Sharina (Janet League), and had pretended to be dead to be with her (a flashback scene, right). This convoluted storyline—Brandon had died on camera in 1979!— afforded actor Keith Charles with his third role on the show. He had previously played Alex McDaniels, Hope Bauer's first love (1976), and Frank Nelson, Kelly's physician father in 1981.

with nurse Hillary Bauer. Claire was a humorless, intense doctor, whose life
had been nothing but disappointments, not the least of which was the decision
of her "roommate" Kelly Nelson to accept a medical assignment in Boston.

Determined not to be vulnerable, Claire tried to keep it strictly business
with Jim, but their long hours together filled Claire with nothing but admira-
tion—and lust—for Dr. Jim. Meanwhile, under the mistaken belief that Jim
had gone to South America to help stop the spread of the virus, Hillary flew
down there and was caught in a quarantine. She was befriended by hard-nosed
reporter Fletcher Reade, and when Hillary came down with the virus, Fletcher
tried everything to get Hillary back to the States for medical treatment. Eventually, thanks to Alan Spaulding, Hillary was smuggled back to Springfield. Jim
found a successful treatment for the Dreaming Death, and Hillary recovered.
Hillary and Jim reaffirmed their love, and Fletcher and Claire, finding two hard
heads are better than one, embarked on a stormy affair.

Alan Spaulding, who had orchestrated Hillary's escape from the jungle,
once again found himself footloose and fancy-free when his beleaguered wife,
Hope, finally got up enough gumption and left him. Alan had been treating
Hope much in the same undermining way that had characterized his marriage
to Elizabeth. He had also resorted to the same kind of ruthless business wheeling
and dealing that Hope had tried to eliminate from Alan's life. Hope's drinking
developed into full-scale alcoholism, but with the help of her uncle Ed, she
recovered. After her divorce, Hope took her son Alan Michael and left town.

Alan tried to hit on one of his executives, Trish Lewis, a moral, responsible
young woman who had kowtowed to her powerful family all her life. Trish
resisted his advances; she was seeing Ross Marler, and, besides, Alan was still
married. But Alan's sexual browbeating got a little too intense and Trish succumbed to his charms one night. She was immediately filled with regrets and
told Alan that he had to honor her relationship with Ross Marler. Furious, Alan
ruined Ross's campaign for district attorney by having him framed for drug
possession. Ross vowed revenge and eventually got it, aided by Alan's own sister.

Alexandra Spaulding von Halkein had been living in Europe for many
years, the wife of a German baron. She returned to Springfield during a mag-
nificent masked ball, and soon she confided to Ross Marler her real reason for
being back in the States. Years before, Alex had had a love affair with Eric
Luvonaczek, a brilliant but indigent concert pianist. The two had a son, whom
they named Brandon after Alex's father. But Brandon Spaulding was certainly
not deserving of this honor, for he schemed to put an end to this "immoral"
affair. Brandon paid off Eric, and Eric deserted Alex, taking little Brandon with
him. Alex spent years looking for them and eventually gave up, finally settling

"Auntie Dearest" Alexandra Spaulding (Beverlee McKinsey) took the town by storm. Nephew Phillip (now played by John Bolger) was alternately amused and horrified by her machinations.

down with Baron von Halkein. But Alex, in disgust, eventually left the baron when his alcoholism and compulsive gambling had wasted away the family fortunes.

Alex was back in Springfield to resume her search for her son. She had always blamed Alan for not interceding on her behalf with their father. Alan had not lifted one finger to help Alex locate her son. So Alex joined forces with Ross to bring Alan to his knees. Alex found proof that Alan was funding the research into the antidote to the Dreaming Death virus so he might sell it to a power-mad group of corporations who planned to keep Third World countries at their mercy. Blackmailed by Alex, Alan signed over all his holdings to his sister and disappeared in a South American jungle to avoid arrest.

Alex took over Alan's mansion and spent her energy trying to locate her long-lost son. With Ross's help, Alex was finally reunited with her son, a streetwise gang leader who called himself Lujack. (Well, have you ever heard of a hood calling himself Brandon Luvonaczek?) Lujack had gotten a job at Tony Reardon's bar, Company, and his contact with Beth Raines brought out a much more sensitive side to his character. Beth encouraged him to leave the Galahads, but Lujack found it difficult to break with the gang, considering them

After her relationship with Phillip went on the rocks, Beth fell in love with Alexandra's streetwise son, Lujack (Vincent Irizarry), 1984.

family. Then there was his ex-girlfriend Darcy, who had a fog-horn voice and all the charm of a Heavy Metal nightmare.

Darcy was violently jealous of Lujack's attention to Beth, and when Lujack tried to break with the gang, Darcy went berserk, holding Beth, Lujack, and Alexandria hostage at Cedars Hospital. After Darcy shot some of the hospital riff-raff, Lujack got her to throw down the gun. Darcy was committed to a mental hospital, and Lujack got the rest of the Galahads jobs at Spaulding Enterprises with the grudging approval of his mother. Lujack also planned a future with Beth Raines, who had given up on Phillip once and, er, for a while.

Phillip, who had seemed to take a page from his father's book, was unable to accept the loss of Beth and plotted to sabotage Lujack's new restaurant. He hired small-time thug Andy Ferris to create problems so the restaurant wouldn't pass the inspection it needed to open. Without Phillip's assent, Andy foolishly set up an explosion, which ended up blinding Beth. Lujack was found criminally negligent, and Beth ironically turned to Phillip for support. But Phillip had

<u>July 27, 1984</u>

Darcy: I know what's really up. You don't like the idea of your girl—your *ex*-girl—taking over your gang, and making it the *top* gang—the *best*.

Lujack: You're dreaming, Darcy.

Darcy: You're the one who's dreaming—or drunk—or out of your mind—if you think for one second you're gonna stop me. (SHE TURNS TOWARD THE GANG, TRYING TO KEEP HER COOL.) Okay, look—I don't know what number Lujack did on you. But I been fooled by him myself, so I ain't gonna hold it against you. I'll give you one more chance. Tell this prep jerk to kiss off—*now*. (DESPERATE.) C'mon guys. We'll have it made after we do our thing to those pigs on the Hill. You don't want to end up a loser like Lujack.

Pretty Boy: We'd get burned for sure with that plan of yours, Darcy.

Trimmer: The task force'd zap us as soon as we got anywhere near the Hill.

Gina: Yeah—and I'd just die if I was sent down the river.

(DARCY LOSES IT. SHE LUNGES AT GINA AND GRABS HOLD OF HER HAIR.)

Darcy: You dumb, worthless broad! Why're ya listening to Lujack. He's the enemy! He's out to trash us. I'm in charge here. You all hear that? *I'm in charge here!*

August 9, 1984

Darcy Holds Cedars Hospital Hostage

Lujack: Remember the goldfish?

Darcy: You crazy or somethin'?

Lujack: We went to the Country Fair, remember.

Darcy: Right, easy marks.

Lujack: I knocked down those wooden milk bottles
           with a softball—the whole pyramid, three
           times.

Darcy: So you're hot stuff.

Lujack: I won a goldfish in one of those little
           plastic bags. I gave it to you. You said
           you never had a pet before.

Darcy: Okay, enough mushy crud.

Lujack: But about a half hour later you got all
           quiet and sad—remember why?

Darcy: They ran outta chocolate sodas?

Lujack: I had to walk you around that stupid ferris
           wheel and finally you told me. You said you
           were sad 'cause the fish wasn't gonna have
           no friends. Like all alone, swimming round
           and round in the same bowl. People staring
           at it through the glass, feeding it, but it
           wouldn't have nobody to care about, and to
           care about *it*, understand it.

Darcy: I'm gonna throw up.

Lujack: I went back and threw that stupid softball
           at that pile of wooden milk bottles for an
           hour, but I got you another fish. 'Cause it
           was important to you. And I know why.

Darcy: (COMING DOWN OFF THE SPEED.) You finished?

Lujack: We both been alone most of our lives,
          Darce. Lots of people around, but we been
          alone.

Darcy: (STARTING TO CRACK.) So what?

Lujack: Then we found the Galahads and we weren't
          alone no more. There were other fish like
          us swimming around together in the bowl.
          People could stare all they wanted. We knew
          each other, we cared about each other. The
          thing is, Darce, I just started to find out
          that us fish don't have to stay in this
          glass bowl. There's a whole ocean out
          there. It's scary and it's big, but that
          doesn't mean we can't make it. We don't
          have to be alone.

Darcy: Easy for you to say.

Lujack: No. It's not. But I jumped outta that bowl.
          You're still swimming around in there. You
          feel deserted. You are *alone*. It's not a
          good feeling. And you're mad. At me. You
          thought we were friends and I left you,
          trapped in that fishbowl all alone. I love
          you, Darcy. I know all about you, and I
          love you. Other people will love you, too.
          You won't be alone. Don't do to yourself
          what you didn't want to have happen to that
          goldfish.

DARCY SUDDENLY TURNS AND GOES INTO LUJACK'S ARMS.
SHE'S SOBBING. GENTLY, HE TAKES THE GUN OUT OF HER
HAND.

Darcy: I wanna die.

Lujack: You're gonna live, Darce. And things are
          gonna get better and you'll never be alone,
          I promise . . . I'm your friend.

gotten himself into a pickle with the beautiful, scheming India von Halkein, Alex's stepdaughter. India bought a tape recording of Phillip with Andy Ferris, and was able to blackmail Phillip into marrying her.

India and Phillip's marriage was a farce, but it had its lusty moments, and they had a begrudging respect for each other's dark side. Beth got her sight back, and she and Lujack tracked Andy Ferris down. Andy confessed and warned them that Alex was covering up for Phillip's partial responsibility in the blast. Beth and Lujack forgave Andy on the condition he would help them get a public confession from Phillip at Alexandra's Valentine's Day party. Andy brought a copy of the incriminating tape to the party, but he seemed nervous and unwilling to go through with the plan. Lujack lost his temper and screamed that if Andy did not proceed, Lujack would kill him. Suddenly, the lights went out and a gunshot was heard. Lujack was arrested and convicted for Andy's murder.

The stormy marriage of Phillip and India (Mary Kay Adams) had its moments, usually of the Fredricks of Hollywood variety, 1985.

After Lujack's conviction, it seemed that India was the killer, since she had managed to sneak the tape out of Alex's home despite a police search. But the real killer turned out to be gentle, mild-mannered Floyd Parker, who had lost his chance to start over. He had not forgiven Andy for blowing up the club and blinding Beth, whom Floyd secretly adored. Floyd kidnapped India and tried to force India to sign a confession, but India was rescued and Floyd was put behind bars. Lujack was set free, but he barely spoke to his mother, since she had been so anxious to protect Phillip and the Spaulding name and reputation.

Reva Shayne Lewis had originally blown into town with the expressed purpose of breaking up her ex-husband Billy's romance with Vanessa Chamberlain. She was being paid by Alan Spaulding, who hoped that Vanessa (and her stocks) would fall into his bed. The plan worked for a while, but Reva was having pangs of conscience—she was a woman of impulse, not deviousness. Reva saw how much Billy and Vanessa loved each other, even though their independent natures kept threatening to split them apart. Reva showed her true colors when she helped Vanessa lock Billy's date to the masked ball in a closet, paving the way for Vanessa and Billy to be married right on the spot!

Afterwards, Reva resumed her interest in Billy's younger brother, Josh. But this romance was frowned upon by Josh's father H.B. Lewis, who blackmailed Reva to stay away from Josh, threatening to tell Josh how far Reva had strayed from that innocent girl from Oklahoma that Josh had loved years before. While H.B. thought Reva was too wild for Josh, she wasn't wild enough for old H.B. So he whisked Reva off to Hawaii for a quickie wedding. When Josh heard, he was so furious that he drove his car crazily, and the car spun out of control crashing into a tree. Josh was left paralyzed from the waist down. Reva and H.B. insisted that Josh move in with them, but Josh was so bitter and obnoxious that Reva thought she would lose her mind. At a country club party, Reva stripped off her clothes, stood in the small fountain in the courtyard, and told Josh to take a good, hard look, because he was always looking at her like she was naked anyway. Afterwards, Josh was much kinder to Reva.

Reva got a lot of moral support from her sister Roxie, who had arrived in Springfield looking for the good life. When she spotted Rick Bauer, Roxie said "That's the man for me," and made a beeline for him. Rick and Mindy fought constantly, and when Rick split up with Mindy, Roxie was there to pick up the pieces. However, a mysterious businessman, Kyle Sampson, threatened to expose Roxie's past as a hooker in Tulsa unless she agreed to use her job at Lewis Oil to get information to help Kyle in his bid to take over the company. Roxie

<u>July 30, 1984</u>

Reva: (MANIAC.) Here I am world! Reva Shayne
            Lewis—tramp, adulteress, scarlet woman!
            How'm I doin', Bud? (JOSH DOES NOT RESPOND.)
            Not enough? O.K., can't disappoint Joshua!
            (RUNS TO FOUNTAIN AND JUMPS IN WADING TO
            MIDDLE AND SPLASHING HERSELF WITH WATER.) I
            baptize myself ''The Slut of Springfield!''
            Isn't that right, Joshua? Isn't that what you
            want people to think of me? Tell everybody to
            come out and watch. (STARTS TO HUM
            ''STRIPPER'' SONG AGAIN AS SHE BUMPS AND
            GRINDS SLIPPING OFF HER STRAPS.) You like
            this, Joshua? Huh!?

Josh: (ANGRY.) Put your clothes on, and get the
            hell out of here.

Reva: (LAUGHS AND SOBS.) Why!? Aren't you
            enjoying' this!? You look at me like I'm
            naked all the time. You don't think I have a
            brain or a heart! All your dirty li'l mind
            sees is my body! So, here it is, Joshua! Take
            a look! Take a good look!

was caught spying and was fired. But she went to Alaska to see Billy Lewis in order to make up for her mistake. She told Billy that Kyle had sent someone to pose as a drilling expert with sabotaged parts to ruin Lewis Oil's drilling operation.

Billy accepted Roxie's help and forgave her while Roxie resolved to confess her entire past life to Rick. Unfortunately, she was in a snowmobile accident that left her with amnesia. To support herself, she took a job in a bordello, calling herself Rosie. As Rosie, she attracted the attention of Kurt Corday, a handsome young oil worker who proposed marriage. Meanwhile, Roxie's sister Reva came to Alaska to search for Roxie. Reva was accompanied by Kyle, who felt guilty about blackmailing Roxie. Kyle and Reva found Roxie, dragged her

Reva Shayne (Kim Zimmer) with "the old poop" himself, H. B. Lewis (Larry Gates), 1984.

The volatile Lewis clan included Mindy (Krista Tesreau), her father, Billy (Jordan Clarke), his wife, Vanessa (Maeve Kinkead), and Billy's sister, Trish (Rebecca Hollen), 1985.

*Kyle Sampson (Larkin Malloy) and the women in his life: Maeve Stoddard
(Leslie Denniston) and the indefatigable Reva (Kim Zimmer), 1985.*

to a private jet against her will, but Kurt Corday jumped aboard and pulled a
gun on Kyle and Reva, forcing the two to parachute off the plane. Roxie returned
to Springfield and remembered her love for Rick, and Kurt eventually found
true love with Mindy. They were married in a beautiful medieval-themed
ceremony.

When Reva and Kyle parachuted from the plane, they landed on the farm
of an Amish couple. The couple gave them room and board in exchange for
farm chores and rebuilding the barn's roof. Reva and Kyle had their first taste
of manual labor, and both took pride in doing something with their hands other
than to sign a check! The serenity of the Amish couple and the farm also forced
Reva to come to terms with her recent unhappy past. After Josh regained the
use of his legs, Reva and Josh realized their love had never died, and made
plans to reconcile. But when H.B. underwent delicate heart surgery, Josh
stepped aside. Reva found herself pregnant, and Josh realized that Reva wanted
to have H.B.'s baby and really did love his father. So Josh left town.

But Reva lost her baby when Vanessa Lewis, stoned on tranquilizers, accidentally hit Reva with her car. Vanessa kicked her drug dependency, but Reva went into a deep depression. Reva finally got out of bed to search for Roxie in Alaska. Now here at the farm, the impulsive Reva found herself falling in love with Kyle, despite the fact that Kyle was supposedly H.B.'s illegitimate son. When Kyle and Reva returned to Springfield, Reva asked H.B. for a divorce. But Kyle had problems with the fact that he was going to marry his father's wife, and Kyle and Reva separated. Kyle slept with an old girl friend Maeve Stoddard, who became pregnant. Out of honor, Kyle married Maeve. But a despondent Reva, feeling that she had lost everything, threw herself off a bridge in a suicide attempt. However, her will to live pulled her through, and with the assistance of reporter Fletcher Reade, who used Reva as the center of a series of articles about suicide, Reva managed to reach out to other people who had become despondent.

Meanwhile, H.B. and his old friend, Kyle's mother, Miss Sally Gleason, decided to stop lying about Kyle being H.B.'s son—Kyle wasn't. In a shocking announcement, Miss Sally and H.B. told Billy that his natural mother wasn't the sainted Miss Martha, but Miss Sally herself! So, Kyle and Billy were brothers after all. At first, Billy and Mindy refused to accept Miss Sally as his mother and her grandmother, but they saw how she loved them and they were reconciled. Miss Sally would do anything to protect Billy—even lie under oath to save him. This became necessary because Billy had become involved with Infinity, a weird power-mad organization which endeavored to take over Sampson Industries.

David Preston, a member of Infinity and supposed friend of Kyle, repeatedly hypnotized Billy with a double-circled emblem, so Billy would shoot Kyle Sampson. Even programmed, Billy could not bring himself to shoot his brother. Instead, David Preston was shot, and Billy stood trial for murder. But thanks to Beth Raines and her new art associate Jackson Freemont, who presented a videotape containing the double ring symbols in court, Billy went into a trance again, and the jury realized that Billy was the victim of a terrible plot, and they exonerated him. Billy's daughter had been charged a co-defendant, and had to spend her wedding night in jail. Their life in some kind of order now, Kurt concentrated on making the bar, Company, a success while Mindy embarked on a career as "The Sampson Girl," representing Sampson products.

However, Mindy and Kurt's fairy-tale marriage soured afterwards. They fought about having children and about her jobs as the Sampson Girl and as a TV aerobics instructor. When Mindy observed Kurt and Roxie in what appeared to be a romantic clinch (actually they had fallen asleep after working on Kurt's dream house) Mindy saw red. She accidentally knocked over a kerosene lantern and fled from the half-finished house. The lantern set fire to the house, and Kurt and Roxie barely got away with their lives. When Mindy finally admitted her culpability months later, Kurt had had enough; he took a job on a Venezuelan oil rig to get away from her.

Beth and Jackson were able to save Billy when they realized that Lujack's musical video held the key. Lujack had seen the Infinity symbol in the warehouse of Delilah records, a subsidiary of Sampson Enterprises. And Beth and Jackson decided to use the symbol as a motif throughout the video, unaware of the harm it would produce. Eventually, Lujack realized the connection between David Preston and Infinity. The organization was cornered, and kidnapped Beth and Jackson. Lujack rescued Beth, but a boiler aboard the Infinity ship exploded. Close to dying at the hospital, Lujack bade a sweet good-bye to his mother and Beth, then passed away.

*Lujack taping his rock
video, 1985.*

Triumphant Mindy took the top prize in the Sampson Girl Contest, 1986. Dick Cavett congratulated, er, embraced the winner.

Alexandra was devastated by the loss of her son, the son with whom she only shared a year. To cover up her pain, Alex refused to deal with it and began plotting against the men she considered her enemies. Complicating her life was the introduction of a handsome blond magician who claimed he was Alex's brother. Alex detested Simon intensely, but one time she caught Simon in the family mausoleum and Simon was weeping at Lujack's grave. From that moment, Alex believed him and accepted Simon as part of the family. Meanwhile, India plotted to get Simon to marry her—she loved the last name Spaulding—but Simon had eyes only for Jesse Matthews, the daughter of Alex's new assistant Calla.

Fletcher Reade suddenly ran off to report on war-torn Beirut. Claire followed and discovered that Fletcher had a three-year-old daughter there who was missing and presumed dead. Fletcher and Claire's best friends, Maureen and Ed Bauer, flew to Lebanon as well to help in the search. While Maureen and Fletcher were looking for any evidence of Fletcher's daughter's death, the

February 3, 1986

(ALEX—STILL FOCUSED ON PHOTO OF LUJACK—TURNS, WALKS
SLOWLY AWAY FROM CALLA. SHE FORGETS CALLA IS EVEN IN
THE ROOM—AS SHE BEGINS TO ADDRESS LUJACK DIRECTLY.)

Alex: I miss being able to look at you, Brandon
           . . . being able to study this first thing
           every morning—and drink in every detail—so
           the memory would be fresh . . . and I could
           carry it with me all through each day. (A
           SMALL, SAD SMILE.) I know. You'd say—Ma—
           what's the story here. You weren't gone *that*
           long. How could you forget my face: That's
           what I thought, too . . . But grief can play
           strange tricks, Darling. One night—when I
           was in bed—about to drift off . . . I started
           to say goodnight to you—the way I've done
           every night since I . . . But when I tried to
           picture you in my mind—I couldn't. Not your
           sweet, dark eyes or hair—not your smile—or
           the way you set your jaw . . . not that look
           you get in your eyes when it seems as though
           you could see right into my soul . . . I tried
           everything to conjure you—but nothing
           worked. Instead, I saw all the others I've
           lost in my life: my father, my brother, Eric,
           Locke. I sat up at that point, shook my head
           to clear it, and concentrated harder. But
           that only made things worse. I started to see
           all my enemies, then . . . all the men who've
           defied me: Kyle Sampson, Billy Lewis, Ross
           Marler. Their faces dissolved in and out of
           each other—over and over and over—filling
           my head—leaving no room for you. I tried to
           block them out, but it was no use. They kept
           coming—they wouldn't let up—they wouldn't
           go away. And then—finally—one last face
           appeared. The worst one of all. It came
           closer and closer—laughing at me the whole
           time . . . *Laughing* at me . . . (HER EYES COLD,
           NOW HER VOICE DEADLY.) The face of . . . him
           . . . Simon.

two were caught in a bombing raid and were feared dead. In their shock and confusion, Ed and Claire turned to each other and wound up spending the night together. But there was another shock for the once close four friends: Claire became pregnant with Ed's child.

Back at Cedars, Ed and Claire's name and reputation were dragged through the mud with the efforts of a bitter nurse, Charlotte Wheaton. Charlotte spread rumors that Ed was drinking on the job, which got him suspended from the hospital. Then she called in to Fletcher and Maureen's radio show, pretending to be a distressed caller, telling the radio audience all the intimate details of Claire's pregnancy by Ed. Everybody at the hospital recognized that Charlotte was talking about Claire and Ed. When Charlotte was found dead, it looked as if Ed and Claire were guilty, and to avoid arrest they went to a nearby town so Claire would not have to have her baby in jail.

But Claire and Ed were caught and brought back to Springfield to be tried for murder. But Fletcher Reade was able to prove the real killer was Charlotte's sister, TV news reporter Alicia Rohmer. Ed and Claire were set free, and Claire gave birth to a baby girl, Michelle. Claire moved in with Maureen for a while and attempted to foist Michelle's care on anybody and everyone. Claire was miserable and was bent on making everyone else's life just as miserable. Ed took Michelle to visit an ailing Bert at Meta's home, and Michelle perked up Bert's spirits immensely.

When Ed returned home with Michelle, he had some sad news: Bert had died in her sleep the night before. Bert's friends gathered and shared their many special memories of her. Bert's death had a profound effect on the entire family. Ashamed of his drug habit, Rick threw down the pills and vowed never to touch them again. Ed and Maureen decided to fight for custody of Michelle. Cracking under professional and personal pressures, Claire went off the deep end, threatening to expose Rick's drug habit and make it very clear to the court that Ed's drinking problem was far from over.When Rick discovered that Claire was about to strike the child, Rick scooped up the baby and brought her to safety.

It was then that Ed vowed to take Michelle away from Claire. He looked at a picture of Bert, then the baby in his arms, and thought, "No Bauer will ever grow up in a home without love."

Claire came totally unglued afterwards, convincing herself that Kyle Sampson loved *her*. She went to Reva Bend to confront Reva with the laughable bulletin that Kyle loved Claire, not Reva. But Claire's timing could not have been worse: Cain Harris, the circus performer who had saved Reva after her attempted suicide, was holding Reva against her will. He had become obsessively in love with Reva, and demanded that she make love to him. Claire interrupted them, and the demented Cain dragged them both to the bridge while holding a gun on them. Fortunately, Kyle and Fletcher came to the rescue: after Cain shot and wounded Fletcher and then tossed Claire off the bridge, Kyle shot and killed Cain.

Unfortunately, Maeve, who was nine months pregnant, witnessed what seemed like a romantic reunion between Reva and Kyle on the bridge afterwards. Maeve had had enough! Feeling that after a divorce the powerful Kyle would be given custody of their child, Maeve went to her friend Dr. Louie Darnell. Louie delivered the child and told everyone that the boy, who was named Ben, was his nephew. Maeve merely told Kyle that the baby had been born dead. Kyle was devastated, but made Maeve's life hell for months to come. He dangled a divorce in front of her—she would only have to sell the *Springfield Journal* to him. And when Maeve wanted to adopt Ben, Kyle threatened Louie with court proceedings for allowing such an "unstable" woman to care for his nephew.

In a confrontation between Reva, Kyle, Fletcher, and Maeve, Reva learned the extent of Kyle's deviousness. Boxed into a corner, Kyle came out exploding with emotional fireworks. If Maeve wanted her divorce, all she would have to do would be to supply a death certificate and tell him where their son was born and where he was buried. Maeve told him as much as she remembered, but said it was too painful to dredge up details of the death of their child. Fletcher, who had fallen in love with Maeve, became suspicious and learned that Ben had been born May 21, 1986—the same night of the shootings at the bridge. Meanwhile, Kyle proposed marriage to Reva, but she tearfully refused: there were too many lies, too much bad history between them to have a happy marriage.

Maeve trusted only Louie and her friend India von Halkein with her secret. India had been secretly skimming funds from the Spaulding Foundation to save her father's castle in Andorra. Arrested at the prodding of her ex-husband Phillip, India was sent to a women's prison where she was befriended by a young girl, Dorie Smith, who was as mischievous and spirited as India herself. India was shocked when she began having maternal feelings for Dorie, and made plans to adopt the tough but adorable young woman. Worried about her father, who was an alcoholic and in ill health, India and Dorie hijacked H.B. Lewis's plane to Andorra, and waiting for them there was a shocker: Alan Spaulding.

Alan had last been seen two years previously running through a South American jungle with bullets ricocheting around him. A mysterious woman nursed him back to health, then he left to fly to Andorra to choreograph his comeback in Springfield. He convinced the Baron von Halkein to let him invest the funds India was sending over. Alan did an excellent job in his investment schemes, and began buying up valuable Springfield properties: a radio and TV station and a newspaper. Alan's reappearance in Springfield rocked the town. Alexandra shifted from pure love for her brother to total mistrust. Phillip felt nothing but bitterness.

Phillip had recently reconciled with Beth, who took a job with an art curator. Unfortunately, this was the same curator to whom India had sent her castle's cornerstone. India knew the cornerstone contained thousands of old gold pieces, and sending the cornerstone to the curator was the only way to get the gold into the country without raising suspicions. The night of its arrival India broke into the museum to claim her family's gold. But the curator had beaten her to it, shot Phillip and took Beth, who had been working late, hostage. He took the gold and Beth to a nearby lake and disappeared. Weeks dragged into months, but Phillip and Lillian never gave up on Beth. She had to be safe. With the help of Reva, Kyle spotted the treasure at the bottom of the lake, and presented it with a great flourish to the Andorran government. Alan and India vowed to retrieve the von Halkein treasure.

Meanwhile Alexandra, finding Alan's sudden wealth suspicious, flew down to San Rios to investigate. Her plane went down in the jungle and she was nursed back to health by the natives. Flying down to San Rios to save her, Simon—who finally admitted that he was not Alex's brother, but Lujack's half-brother, the son of Eric Luvonaczek—and pilot Johnny Bauer, Rick's second cousin, discovered that they had a stowaway: Jesse!

Calla was furious; she detested Simon and disapproved totally of Jesse's romance with Simon. This caused great problems in Calla's relationship with Ross Marler. Ross found it very difficult to approve of Calla's constant smothering of Jesse and Calla's outrageous social ambition. But Calla also faced a secret threat. Vanessa Lewis discovered that the child she had given up for adoption seventeen years before might be Jesse!

Coming out of her coma after many months, Claire admitted that she had crazily, spitefully given Rick an "F" on his medical board tests without even reading the paper. The board, over the objections of Alan Spaulding, whose feud with the Bauers went back many years, gave Rick the opportunity to take the exam over again. Unfortunately, Rick accidentally was given two sleeping pills instead of two aspirins for his headache, and he slaved to get through the arduous exam. But Bauer Power pulled him through: Rick passed his exam and became a doctor, fulfilling the dreams of his namesake, great-grandfather Frederick Bauer, who had come to America as a penniless immigrant fifty years before.

Bert, who practically raised Rick, would have been so proud. With a big grin Rick looked skyward and said, "Thanks, Grandma."

To Be Continued . . . **6**

In their quest to locate Alexandra, Simon and Jesse immediately ran into trouble in San Rios with Tito, a mysterious revolutionary who hated Alan Spaulding. Tito held Simon, Jesse, and Alex hostage, demanding that Alex contact her brother Alan to negotiate their release. Meanwhile, just as Ross Marler and Johnny Bauer prepared to rescue the trio, Vanessa Lewis ran onto the runway and demanded that she be taken along. Ross pushed the hysterical Vanessa off the plane, but not before Vanessa screamed that she had given birth to a daughter eighteen years before and given her up for adoption. Vanessa had every reason to believe that Jesse was her daughter—and Jesse's father was none other than Ross Marler!

In San Rios, Ross and Johnny rescued the three and brought them safely back to Springfield. Ross found out from Calla that Calla was the natural mother of Jesse, so Jesse couldn't possibly be his and Vanessa's child. But Vanessa and Ross's new closeness drove a wedge in Vanessa and Billy's marriage, and Billy moved out. Vanessa and Ross continued to search for their child and finally found her, after many dead ends, right under their very nose: *Their* natural daughter was Dinah Morgan, who had been turned over to an adoption agency by Gordon Matthews, Calla's ex-husband.

In Springfield, Jesse began to assert herself, and broke up with Simon. She had spent her entire life under the thumb of her mother Calla and was smothered by Simon's overprotectiveness. She needed to be on her own for a while, so she moved into Bea Reardon's boarding house. Bea also welcomed her daughter, Chelsea (who had been a successful singer in New York) back home. But tragedy struck soon for Chelsea: when she went to pick up her fiancé at the airport, he was inebriated and insisted on driving. At the same time, Phillip was driving Dinah home from a party, and the two cars collided. Chelsea's fiancé was killed, but Chelsea vowed to go on with her life and began singing again at Company.

Phillip's father, Alan, was up to his usual manipulations. Worried over Phillip's declining physical and emotional health, Alan hired a coroner to claim that an unidentified corpse was Beth (it was not). Beth was declared legally dead, and Alan was pleased that Phillip seemed finally to be going on with his life. Meanwhile, Alex continued to investigate Alan's past. There was much more to Alan's stay in San Rios a few years back, and Alex vowed to find out what it was. But India grew closer to Alan when he turned over to her the deed to the von Halkein castle. India's father moved back into his home with Sophia.

At the hospital, a new physician, Dr. Mark Jarrett, created quite a splash with his unorthodox medical practices. Jarrett had been drummed out of hospital after hospital, and Ed Bauer, the chief of staff, totally mistrusted him. But Claire Ramsey had immense faith in Jarrett and Jarrett—over Ed's objections— performed successful laser brain surgery on Claire. Afterwards, Ed accepted Jarrett as an innovative, if abrasive, part of the staff.

Meanwhile, Kyle insisted that he was a changed man, and Reva began weakening toward him. She remembered the simple but beautiful life they had shared at the Amish farm. After a heart-to-heart talk with her friend Fletcher, Reva agreed to be Kyle's wife. At the same time, Maeve confessed to Fletcher that Ben was her natural son. Fletcher accepted her deception and urged Maeve to get her divorce from Kyle as soon as possible. As Maeve flew to Mexico to secure her divorce, Kyle and Reva made wedding plans.

Maeve had left Ben in the hands of a babysitter while she was gone. When Kyle found out that Louie Darnell was also out of town, Kyle began to worry about Ben. He found out that Louie and Maeve had no adoption applications on file, and took legal action to protect the child. When Maeve heard about this in Mexico, she struggled to get back to Springfield, but she fell deathly ill south of the border. Fletcher rushed to her side.

When Maeve and Fletcher returned, Maeve burst into the church where Kyle and Reva were exchanging vows. Maeve interrupted the ceremony and demanded to know where Ben was. Upset, Reva ran from the church. Just as Reva was about to be hit by a car, she was pushed out of the way by a strangely familiar man. It was Reva's ex-lover, Josh, whom she hadn't seen in two years. He scooped her up and brought her to safety. It was clear from their glances that their love affair was far from over. . .

Lynne Adams

Leslie Jackson Bauer

Although Lynne had thought of a career in teaching, her interest in acting went back to her parents, Rosilind Gould and Robert K. Adams, both of whom had roles on *Guiding Light* when the show was on radio. So it was natural that Lynne follow in her parents' footsteps and be selected over nine hundred actresses in 1966 to play the pivotal role of Leslie, who would marry first Ed, then Mike Bauer. She left the show in 1971 to play Amy Ames on *The Secret Storm* for two years, then returned to her part on *Guiding Light* until Leslie's untimely death in 1976.

Grant Aleksander

Phillip Spaulding

Although Grant was on the show for only two years, his impact will not soon be forgotten. He attended prep school and was planning a career in professional sports, probably football, before the acting bug bit him. At Washington and Lee University in Virginia, he starred in numerous plays, then took off for New York. The six-foot-one-inch, 175-pound actor soon found work as a model, then joined the show in December 1982 as the rich, self-destructive Phillip. The popular actor later decided to leave after two years, later guesting in a segment of *Who's the Boss?* and joining the cast of the west coast soap *Capitol* as the slippery D.J. Phillips.

Millette Alexander

Dr. Sara McIntyre

Prior to joining *Guiding Light* in January 1969, Millette had a long and varied career on television and in theater. After studying with Lee Strasberg, she was seen on Broadway in *Come Blow Your Horn* and *Jason and Medea*. Her soap career began in 1958 as elusive commercial artist Gail Armstrong on *The Edge of Night*. In 1961 she was seen as gun moll Gloria Saxon on *From these Roots* which was followed by a two-year stint as Sylvia Hill on *As the World Turns*. Afterwards, Millette returned to *The Edge of Night* for two more roles, as Laura Hillyer and her look-alike Julie Jamison. Her thirteen-year run on *Guiding Light* ended in 1982.

Lisa Brown

Nola Reardon

Multitalented Lisa began her career as part of the dance-and-drill team of the Kansas City Chiefs, then toured with Pearl Bailey in *Hello Dolly*. In New York, she landed a featured role in *The Best Little Whorehouse in Texas*, where she was spotted by Douglas Marland, who created the role in February 1980 of Nola Reardon for her on *Guiding Light*. In August 1982, at the height of her popularity, she assumed the lead role in the hit Broadway musical *42nd Street* and played the two roles concurrently. After marrying her co-star Tom Nielsen, who played Floyd Parker, Lisa left *Guiding Light* in 1985 and popped up as Iva Snyder on *As the World Turns*.

Ed Bryce

Bill Bauer

After a stint with the 99th Bomber Group in Italy during World War II, Ed studied acting at Columbia University and made appearances on Broadway in *The Cradle Will Rock, Darkness at Noon*, and *The Liar*. Tapped in 1959 to play the alcoholic Bill, Ed found that, out of storyline necessities, he would be written in and out of *Guiding Light* during the next twenty-five years. He popped up in 1977, then reprised the role in 1983. The actor's other soap roles include Bruce Edwards on *The Secret Storm* in 1956, gangster Al King on *Love of Life* in 1958, and Carol Demming's father on *As the World Turns* from 1970 to 1972. Ed's son, Scott Bryce, has played Craig Montgomery on *As the World Turns* since 1982.

Marsha Clark

Hillary Bauer

Marsha is that rare bird: a soap fan who made it big in daytime drama. As president of the Gerald Gordon Fan Club (Nick Bellini, *The Doctors*), she got her foot in the door and even *Daytime TV* magazine followed Marsha as she made the auditioning rounds. She had bit roles on *The Doctors, As the World Turns*, and *Search for Tomorrow*. In December 1978 Marsha got her big break, replacing Linda McCullough as Hillary on *Guiding Light*. Over the next five years, Marsha won a wide following for the special comedic spunk she brought to the role. After leaving *Guiding Light*, she was seen briefly as Tina Clayton on *One Life to Live*.

Kathleen Cullen

Amanda Wexler Spaulding

After attending Loyola University and Mundelin College with degrees in speech and theater, Kathleen came to New York and studied acting at the Herbert Berghof Studios and dance with Alvin Ailey. She was featured in many theater productions, including *Play It Again, Sam, Lovers and Others Strangers*, and *The Fantasticks*. She played fan favorite Amanda Wexler Middleton McFarren Spaulding from July 1978 until August 1983. She and her husband, attorney Tim Baker, have a daughter, Alexis, born in 1981.

Ellen Demming

Meta Bauer Banning

While still in high school Ellen was part of the pioneering days of television broadcasting when she appeared in numerous playlets on the experimental GE station in Schenectady. She studied acting with the celebrated Maude Adams and appeared for seven years in various summer stock groups. She then worked on television in such shows as *Robert Montgomery Presents, Alcoa Theatre*, and *Lamp Unto My Feet*. She took over the role of Meta in January 1953 and stayed with the show for over two decades. Today she lives in upstate New York with her husband, TV producer Hal Thompson.

Susan Douglas

Kathy Roberts Holden

When Susan arrived in the U.S. from Czechoslovakia during World War II she had two strikes against her: an unpronounceable name and no knowledge of English. A year later, she had changed her last name to Douglas, and her knowledge of English was so good that she began to get radio roles in such shows as *Backstage Wife, Nora Drake*, and *The Romance of Helen Trent*. She married Czech concert singer Jan Rubes and joined the cast of *Guiding Light* on radio in 1950 as troubled teen Kathy Roberts. Over the next eight years, Susan raised hell as Kathy, and TV fans were furious with creator Irna Phillips when Susan and her character were written out in 1958.

Judi Evans

Beth Raines

Born in Los Angeles, Judi spent her first eight years on the road, traveling with her parents who worked in a circus. Her father was a trapeze artist and an occasional ringmaster. Judy was drafted at age two to become a baby clown. She attended Pasadena City College, studied acting, and earned money by modeling and appearing in commercials. The role of shy, abused Beth Raines, which she originated in May 1983, was her first television role. For her performance Judi nabbed an Emmy for Supporting Actress in the 1983–84 season. She left the show in July 1986.

Bernard Grant

Dr. Paul Fletcher

After appearing on such radio shows as *Road of Life, Hilltop House*, and *Gangbusters*, Bernie Grant branched out to television and joined the *Guiding Light* cast in May 1956. While on the show Bernie became well known in the business for dubbing foreign films. It was his voice speaking English for such stars as Vittorio Gassman, Yves Montand, and Rossano Brazzi. After a fifteen-year stint with the show, Bernie immediately stepped into the role of Steve Burke on *One Life to Live* as the newspaperman who married Victoria Lord. He remained on that show for five years.

Mart Hulswit

Dr. Ed Bauer

Along with Don Stewart and Michael Zaslow, Mart was one of the show's extremely popular leading men during the seventies. A multilingual actor, he studied at the American Academy of Dramatic Arts and then joined Joseph Papp's New York Shakespeare Festival where he ran the gamut of Shakespearean roles. On prime-time TV he guest-starred on such series as *Mannix, Dr. Kildare*, and *Combat*. His film credits include *Loving*, where he gave a memorable performance as an obnoxious party guest pestering George Segal. After leaving *Guiding Light* Mart appeared briefly on a number of soaps, most notably as the lucky (?) man who married man-hungry Opal Gardner and squired her off *All My Children*. He played Ed on *Guiding Light* from 1969 to 1981.

Vincent Irizarry

Lujack

Fan sensation Vincent, who created the pugnacious Lujack in November 1983, began his career with a scholarship to the Lee Strasberg Theatre Institute. He studied classical piano for six years and appeared in many theater productions, including *Lennon* playing the role of Paul McCartney. (Wasn't that good casting?!) He was seen in the Jameson Parker film *A Small Circle of Friends* and played Sissy Spacek's husband in *Marie: A True Story*. In an amusing sidelight to Vincent's two-year, action-packed role on *Guiding Light*, the actor claimed that the ratings of the show went up when he came aboard because all his Italian relatives started watching!

Lenore Kasdorf

Rita Stapleton Bauer

An army brat, Lenore traveled with her family all over the world and graduated from high school in Bangkok, Thailand. Returning to the U.S., Lenore landed work in commercials and guest parts on such shows as *The Streets of San Francisco, Ironside*, and *Starsky and Hutch*. She joined *Guiding Light* as the sensual, self-serving Rita in October 1975. She stayed with the show until 1981. Married to actor Phil Peters, Lenore moved to the West Coast and played Dr. Veronica Kimball on *Days of Our Lives* in 1983. She later guest-starred in an episode of *Moonlighting*.

James Lipton

Dr. Dick Grant

Guiding Light's matinee idol of the fifties, James Lipton worked extensively in radio before joining the show. Shortly afterwards, he married actress Nina Foch and began writing in his spare time. On Broadway, he was seen in *Dark Legend* and Lillian Hellman's *The Autumn Garden*. After he left *Guiding Light* he served as headwriter for many soaps including *Another World, The Edge of Night, The Doctors* (Emmy nominated) and his old stomping ground *Guiding Light*. He also wrote films and TV movies, recently *Cococabana* starring Barry Manilow. In February 1986, he became headwriter of *Capitol*.

Fran Myers

Peggy Scott Thorpe

Fran started her career at eight, working the dying days of radio soaps in the serial *The Couple Next Door*. The youngster joined the show in May 1965 and practically grew up on the air. She completed her education while still on the show and worked off Broadway and appeared in guest shots on *Play of the Week* and *Route 66*. In May 1975, she married Roger Newman, who had played Ken Norris on *Guiding Light*. After leaving the show in 1979, Fran and Roger tried their hands at writing and are currently associate writers for *Another World*.

Lynne Rogers

Marie Wallace Grant

Lynne's early interest in graphic arts certainly came in handy when she was cast as artist Marie Wallace in December 1954, a part which she would stay with until 1962. Before her stint on *Guiding Light* she played summer stock at the Provincetown Playhouse and numerous roles on radio and television. Afterwards, Marie had a number of soap roles and substituted for Eileen Fulton as Lisa on *As the World Turns* several times. In 1979, she published a book, *The Loves of Their Lives*, which profiled dozens of soap stars and provided a fascinating peek into behind-the-scenes television.

Elvera Roussel

Hope Bauer Spaulding

As a youngster, Elvera traveled extensively and lived in Africa, South Vietnam, Germany, and Laos, countries where her father was a consultant for the Agency for International Development. In the U.S. Elvera performed in regional theater, then made guest appearances on *Police Story, The Brady Bunch*, and *Fantasy Island*. After short stints with *As the World Turns* and *Search for Tomorrow*, she joined *Guiding Light* on March 19, 1979 and won a loyal following over the next four years.

Stefan Schnabel

Dr. Stephen Jackson

One of the busiest actors in the business, Stefan has appeared in thousands of radio broadcasts (including Orson Welles's original *War of the Worlds*); dozens of Broadway shows (*The Three Penny Opera* and *Julius Caesar*) and movies; and over a thousand prime-time TV shows (including thirty-nine half-hour German lessons on PBS). The actor was born in Germany, but when Hitler came to power, Stefan went to England and worked in the Old Vic Theater in London. In 1937, he came to the U.S. and began his prolific career in radio. He joined the cast of *Guiding Light* in 1965 and stayed with the show until 1981.

John Wesley Shipp

Dr. Kelly Nelson

Guiding Light's reigning heartthrob of the early eighties, John moved to New York, studied with Julie Bovasso at LaMama Theater, and got walk-on parts on *All My Children* and *One Life to Live*. After joining the show as Kelly in February 1980, John recorded his first album, *Images*, and appeared opposite Susan Lucci on *Fantasy Island*. When the six-foot-one-inch, 170-pound actor left the show in 1984, he did TV (*Summer Fantasy*) and theater work on the West Coast, but returned to New York in 1985 to give a chilling performance as psychotic killer Douglas Cummings on *As the World Turns*, for which he won an Emmy in 1986.

Don Stewart

Mike Bauer

At age twenty-four Don was the youngest aircraft commander in the Strategic Air Command. Returning to civilian life, he understudied Robert Goulet in *Camelot*, sang the lead in *The Student Gypsy* on Broadway, and starred off-Broadway in *The Fantasticks*. On TV, he made guest appearances on *Adam-12*, *Dragnet*, and *The Virginian*. In December 1968, Don joined the cast of *Guiding Light*. Over the next fifteen years, he proved to be one of the few daytime stars with staying power, appearing on *Daytime TV* magazine's monthly readers poll more than any other *Guiding Light* actor.

Michael Zaslow

Roger Thorpe

Before his smashing nine-year performance as Roger Thorpe (1971–80), the villain with a finger in every storyline pie, Mike had a running role on *Star Trek* for a couple of years, then played Dick Hart on *Search for Tomorrow* and Dr. Peter Chernak on *Love is a Many Splendored Thing*. While on *Guiding Light*, Mike performed in *Fiddler on the Roof* on Broadway and the Broadway revival of *Cat on a Hot Tin Roof* opposite Elizabeth Ashley. Afterwards, he starred in the film *You Light up My Life* and the prime-time serial *King's Crossing*. He returned to daytime in 1983 as international spy David Renaldi on *One Life to Live*.

Who's Who On Guiding Light *8*

Mary Kay Adams

India von Halkein

Mary Kay began her theatrical training at Carnegie-Mellon University then earned her B.F.A. at Emerson College, winning the 1983 Carol Burnett Award. Her theater roles have included Catherine in *Suddenly, Last Summer*, Lucy in *The Rivals*, and major roles in *Henry V, The Merchant of Venice*, and *A Midsummer Night's Dream* with the American Shakespeare Repertory in New York. She began as the high-powered, sophisticated India in August 1984. Mary Kay is a descendent of Presidents John and John Quincy Adams.

Patricia Barry

Sally Gleason

One of the best-known actresses in the business, Pat has appeared on more than eight hundred television series, including *Perry Mason, Gunsmoke, Ben Casey, 77 Sunset Strip, Maverick*, and *Three's Company*. For her work, she has received five Emmy nominations. Her daytime experience goes all the way back to 1954 when she starred in the short-lived soap *First Love* opposite Val Dufour. Since then she has played Addie Horton on *Days of Our Lives*, Viola Brewster on *For Richer, For Poorer*, and Peg English (also known as "Cobra") on *All My Children*. She created the role of the colorful madam Miss Sally in 1984.

Christopher Bernau

Alan Spaulding

Before tackling the plum role of charming, manipulating Alan Spaulding, Chris was one of the busiest actors on the New York stage, appearing in *Sweet Bird of Youth, The Boys in the Band, The Real Inspector Hound*, and other shows. Concurrent with his *Guiding Light* role, he played the title role in *The Passion of Dracula* on Broadway, and starred in the film version for Showtime Cable. Soap fans will remember him from his stint as Phillip Todd on *Dark Shadows* in the sixties. Chris played Alan from 1977 to 1984, and returned to the show in May 1986.

John Bolger

Phillip Spaulding

John certainly had his work cut out for him, replacing the enormously popular Grant Aleksander as Phillip in January 1985. However, he soon won over the fans with his matinee idol looks and ingratiating performance. Concurrent with his *Guiding Light* role, John starred in the highly praised cult film, *Parting Glances*. He is married to opera singer Christine Radman and father of four-year-old Marie Theresa.

Warren Burton

Warren Andrews

Warren has appeared off and on Broadway, but is best known for work with two other Upstairs at the Downstairs alumni: Joan Rivers in her film *Rabbit Test* and TV movie *The Girl Most Likely To . . .*, and Lily Tomlin in three of her TV specials. He received a Grammy Award for contributing material to Lily's comedy album, *This is a Recording*. On daytime TV, Warren has made a career out of playing manipulative businessmen. He received an Emmy for his performance as Eddie Dorrance on *All My Children*, then played Jason Dunlap on *Another World* for two years before joining *Guiding Light* in May 1983.

Jordan Clarke

Billy Lewis

After graduating from Cornell University with degrees in philosophy and acting, Jordan was active in regional theater before joining *Guiding Light* as Dr. Tim Ryan in January 1975. After a year, Jordan moved to the West Coast and appeared on *M*A*S*H, Three's Company, Knightrider*, and in the mini-series *The Executioner's Song* and *Testimony of Two Men*. In May 1983, Jordan became one of the rare performers to return to a soap in a different role, this time around as oil man Billy Lewis.

Leslie Denniston

Maeve Stoddard

Leslie is remembered by soap fans as Karen Peters on *As the World Turns*, where the mysterious Karen came between rivals Dr. John Dixon and Dr. Bob Hughes. Off screen, she married Don Hastings who has played Bob Hughes for over a quarter of a century. Afterwards, Leslie concentrated on musical roles, appearing on Broadway in such shows as *Shenandoah* and *Copperfield*. She is a familiar face in commercials, was seen off Broadway in *The Umbrellas of Cherbourg*, and was featured in the cable TV production of *Pippin*. She joined *Guiding Light* in August 1985.

Kristi Ferrell

Roxie Shayne

Texas-bred Kristi performed with the Dallas Cowboys Cheerleaders for two years, which included the 1979 Super Bowl. She was featured in the first *Dallas Cowboys Cheerleaders* TV movie, then moved to California to model and study acting. She got parts on *Dallas, Chips*, and *Bare Essence*. Afterwards, she won the role of Roxie in September 1984 and moved to New York.

Larry Gates

H.B. Lewis

Veteran actor Larry Gates made his Broadway debut in 1939 in *Speak of the Devil*. His Broadway credits include *First Monday in October*, with Henry Fonda, and *A Case of Libel*, for which he earned a Tony Award nomination. His first movie was the 1952 *Francis Covers the Big Time*. His thirty other films include *Cat on a Hot Tin Roof, Funny Lady*, and *In the Heat of the Night*. On daytime, he appeared on *A World Apart*, and before his current stint as H.B. (starting in August 1983), he played Ira Newton on *Guiding Light* in 1969. He won an Emmy as Outstanding Supporting Actor for his role of H.B. in the 1984–85 season.

Charles Jay Hammer

Fletcher Reade

Jay was a regular on the sitcom *The Jeffersons* as Jenny Willis's white half brother and had a recurring role on the police series *The Blue Knight*. His other TV roles include guest shots on *Mannix, Kojak*, and *Adam-12*. On daytime, he played Max Dekker on the short-lived *Texas*, where he met Pamela Long, who played Ashley Linden on the show. They married soon thereafter. Pamela Long Hammer became headwriter on *Guiding Light* and created the role of Fletcher in March 1984—a role which was supposed to last only a day. But the writers and producers sensed further possibilities for the character and Jay signed a long-term contract.

Maeve Kinkead

Vanessa Chamberlain Lewis

An Emmy nominee for the 1984–85 season as Outstanding Supporting Actress for her *Guiding Light* role, Maeve attended Radcliffe and Harvard. Afterwards, she acted mostly in classical roles in repertory in London, her credits including *The Rivals, Peer Gynt*, and *The Three Sisters*. On daytime, Maeve played Angie Perrini on *Another World* from 1977–80. She married Harry Streep, actress Meryl Streep's brother, on New Year's Eve 1980. The Streeps have two children, Abraham and Maude. She joined *Guiding Light* in June 1980.

Lisby Larson
Calla Matthews

Multi-talented Lisby began her career in New York by landing the lead in the off-Broadway revival of *The Boys from Syracuse*. She did commercials (she was a dancing bottle of salad dressing in one, a Velveeta cheesebox in another), then joined the cast of *Search for Tomorrow* as reporter Victoria Parker. That stint brought her to the attention of other daytime producers, and she was part of the premiere cast of *Texas* in 1980. Over the next two years, Lisby became a daytime favorite as the alternately vixenish and vulnerable Paige Marshall. After a starring role on Broadway in the musical *Five O'Clock Girl*, Lisby played villainess Vanessa Crane on the cable soap *The Catlins*, then joined *Guiding Light* as Calla in October 1985.

Larkin Malloy
Kyle Sampson

Early in Larkin's career, he was the recipient of the New York State Drama Festival's Best Actor Award. In New York, he played off-Broadway in *The Cherry Orchard, The Taming of the Shrew, Ten Little Indians*, and *The Crucible*. In 1980, he originated the role of Sky Whitney on *The Edge of Night*, for which he received an Emmy nomination as Outstanding Actor. When *The Edge of Night* went off the air in December 1984, Larkin joined the cast of *Guiding Light* as Kyle Sampson, Billy Lewis's half brother.

Beverlee McKinsey

Alexandra Spaulding

One of the most respected actresses in television, Beverlee began her daytime drama career as Martha Donnelly in the 1970–71 season on *Love is a Many Splendored Thing*. After a bit part on *Another World*, she returned to create the colorful Iris Carrington on the same show in 1972. For her many exquisite performances, Beverlee was nominated four times for an Outstanding Actress Emmy. In 1980, her popular character was spun off in a new serial, *Texas*, where she received an unusual billing for a daytime actress: *Texas*—starring Beverlee McKinsey. In February 1984, she joined the cast of *Guiding Light*, reuniting her with the *Texas* team of writer Pamela Long Hammer and executive producer Gail Kobe.

Michael O'Leary

Rick Bauer

Michael studied television production at California State University and acting with the celebrated Stella Adler and Milton Katselas. Beginning his professional career in commercials, Michael appeared on such series as *T.J. Hooker, The Greatest American Hero, Gimme a Break*, and the daytime serial *General Hospital*. He also had roles in two movies, *The Killing Touch* and *Lovely but Deadly*. He joined *Guiding Light* in May 1983, delighting TV audiences with his comedic flair and fan club audiences with his wicked impressions of such GL favorites as Phillip and Lujack.

Ellen Parker

Maureen Reardon Bauer

Ellen was born in Paris and grew up in Westchester County, New York. After receiving her fine arts degree at Bard College, she was seen on Broadway in *Plenty* and *Equus* and on TV in the PBS special *Uncommon Women* and the NBC mini-series *Kennedy*. She joined the cast of *Guiding Light* in the spring of 1986, moonlighting for the first three months in the Wallace Shawn play *Aunt Dan and Lemmon*.

Susan Pratt

Dr. Claire Ramsey

After training with the American Academy of Dramatic Arts, Susan appeared on such series as *Baretta, The Streets of San Francisco, Welcome Back, Kotter*, and *The Nancy Drew Murders*. From 1978 to 1982 Susan played nurse Anne Logan—Port Charles's oldest virgin and resident ice princess—on *General Hospital*. While in California she met her husband, Alfredo Pecora. The Pecoras have a daughter, Sophia. Susan created the role of Claire in July 1983.

William Roerick

Henry Chamberlain

Bill Roerick's stage credits span four decades of Broadway history. Among them, *Dear Charlie*, with Tallulah Bankhead; *Tonight at 8:30* with Gertrude Lawrence; *Romeo and Juliet* with Katherine Cornell; *Hamlet* with John Gielgud; and *Medea* with Dame Judith Anderson. His film credits include *A Separate Peace, Day of the Dolphins*, and *The Love Machine*. On daytime TV, Bill played Col. Theodore Adams on the short-lived soap about astronauts, *The Clear Horizon*. He played Dr. Bruce Banning on *Guiding Light* in the early seventies before joining the cast once again in June 1980 as Henry Chamberlain.

Gil Rogers

Hawk Shayne

Before tackling the role of Hawk in September 1985, Gil was best known to audiences as mad-dog Ray Gardner on *All My Children* from 1977 to 1979 with a brief reprise of his role in 1982. (How in the world could Ray and Opal have such stunning kids?) Off Broadway, Gil has been seen in *Come Back, Little Sheba* and on Broadway in *The Great White Hope* and *The Best Little Whorehouse in Texas*. He recently re-created his role as Sheriff Ed Earl Dodd in *Whorehouse* at the Burt Reynolds Theatre in Jupiter, Florida. His films include *Panic in Needle Park* and *Eddie Macon's Run*.

Peter Simon

Dr. Ed Bauer

Peter began his daytime drama career in 1969 as Scott Phillips on *Search for Tomorrow*, where he met his future wife, Courtney Sherman, who played Kathy Parker, his wife on the show. (Courtney, now an associate writer for *Santa Barbara*, is also a *Guiding Light* alumna: she played Dinah Buckley in the 1970–71 season.) After eight years on *Search*, Peter returned to daytime television as the sophisticated Ian McFarland on *As the World Turns* in the 1979–80 season. The next year he joined the cast of *Guiding Light* in the pivotal role of Ed Bauer. He played the role until 1984, left to concentrate on playwriting, and returned to the show in August 1986.

Tina Sloan

Lillian Raines

Remember Tina on *Somerset*? She played sexy, rotten-to-the-core Kate Cannell from 1974 to 1976—a far cry from her current role as kind Nurse Lillian on *GL* which she began in May 1983. Tina's other daytime roles have been as one of the million Patti Whitings on *Search for Tomorrow* and as Dr. Olivia Delaney on *Another World* in the 1981–82 season. Tina has also appeared off Broadway in productions of *Blithe Spirit* and *The Song of Bernadette*.

Rebecca Staab

Jesse Matthews

Rebecca was perfect casting for Jesse Matthews, the perennial beauty pageant contestant. While attending college, Rebecca won the title of Miss Nebraska and went on to compete in the Miss USA pageant in 1980. Afterwards, she went to Paris and began a modeling career which she continues in New York with the Ford Model Agency between acting jobs. Just two months after arriving in Manhattan, Rebecca won a recurring role on *Loving*, then joined the cast of *GL* in October 1985.

Krista Tesreau

Mindy Lewis

Krista was born in St. Louis, Missouri, where she later was declared the winner of the state Miss Teen pageant. An accomplished pianist, Krista was also the winner of the nationwide Liberace Talent Search and the Jefferson City Concerto Competition. On TV, she has appeared on *Kid's World, Happy New Year, America,* and *Circus of the Stars*. The petite (five feet three inches, one hundred pounds) actress joined *Guiding Light* as the spoiled Melinda Sue Lewis in May 1983.

Shawn Thompson

Simon Hall

Although his role of magician Simon is Canadian-born Shawn's first foray into American television, he is well known in his native country as the host of the Sunday morning talk show *Switchback*, described as a "David Letterman for teens." His relatively short tenure on *Guiding Light* has resulted in *Coming Attractions* naming him Performer of the Year—the person the magazine predicts will most likely be the next superstar. Shawn is the first daytime drama performer to be so honored.

Jerry verDorn

Ross Marler

South Dakota-born Jerry attended college with plans to be an English teacher, but found himself fascinated by theater. In 1977, he was invited to appear at Rutgers University as a guest artist in a production of Eric Bentley's play *Are You Now or Have You Ever Been?*. After eleven weeks, it reached Broadway featuring a series of guest actresses playing Lillian Hellman: Liza Minnelli, Dina Merrill, Louise Lasser, and many others. Concurrently with the former play, he played the lead of Shaw's *Man and Superman* for three months at matinee performances. Jerry, who joined *Guiding Light* in March 1979, is married and has two sons.

Michael Wilding, Jr.

Jackson Freemont

The son of Elizabeth Taylor and British matinee idol Michael Wilding, Michael's theatrical credits include Harold Pinter's *Betrayal*, Sam Shepard's *Cowboy Mouth* in London, *Crisis in the Bedroom*, and *La Ronde*. He was featured in the mini-series *A.D.* on TV and co-starred in the movie *Blame It on the Night*. Michael joined *Guiding Light* in June 1985 as Jackson Freemont, a record producer and artist.

Kim Zimmer

Reva Shayne

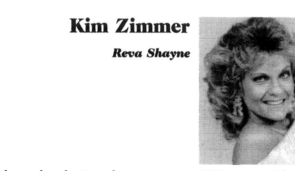

Kim began her daytime drama career in 1978 on *One Life to Live* playing Bonnie Harmer, a political terrorist. The next year she took over the pivotal role of Nola Dancy Aldrich on *The Doctors* from Kathleen Turner, an actress coincidentally Kim later starred with in the movie *Body Heat*. When *The Doctors* was cancelled New Year's Eve 1982, Kim returned to *One Life to Live* to create a new character, the mysterious Echo DiSavoy. After that stint, she joined the cast of *Guiding Light* as Reva in November 1983, and her emotionally packed performance resulted in an Emmy for Outstanding Actress in the 1984–85 season.

Cast and Production Credits   9

Radio Cast 1937–52*

Dr. John Ruthledge	Arthur Peterson (1937–46)
Mary Ruthledge	Mercedes McCambridge (1937–39)
	Sarajane Wells (1939–44)
	Vivian Fridell (1942)
Ned Holden	Ed Prentiss (1937–47)
	John Hodiak (1941)
	Ned LeFevre (1944)
Fredrika Lang	Peggy Fuller (1937–39)
	Muriel Brenner (1939–40)
Torchy Reynolds Holden	Gladys Heen (1939–42)
	Dorothy Reynolds (1942)
Ellen, the housekeeper	Henrietta Tedro (1937–41)
Jacob Kransky	Seymour Young (1937–42)
Rose Kransky	Ruth Bailey (1937–42)
	Louise Fitch (1942)
	Charlotte Manson (1942–43)
Mrs. Kransky	Mignon Schreiber (1937–43)
Rev. Tom Bannion	Frank Behrens (1938–39)

* For editorial purposes, the cast list for radio has been cut off at 1952. From that date until 1956, the show was broadcast on both radio and television.

Laura Martin	Gail Henshaw (1940)
Iris March	Betty Arnold (1939–42)
Eileen O'Brien	Lucy Tedrow (1939)
Spike Wilson	Frank Dane (1937–38)
Clifford Foster	Bret Morrison (1939)
Ethel Foster	Sunda Love (1939)
Jack Felzer	Paul Barnes (1940)
Charles Cunningham	Willis Bouchey (1937–41)
Helene Cunningham	Lesley Woods (1939–41)
Celeste Cunningham	Carolyn McKay (1937–41)
Edward Greenman	Reese Taylor (1942)
	Ken Griffin (1942–43)
Norma Greenman	Eloise Kummer (1942–43)
Ronnie Greenman	Norma Jean Ross (1942)
Joan Greenman	Cheer Brentson (1942)
	Beverly Ruby (1942–43)
Nancy Stewart	Laurette Fillbrandt (1942)
Iris Marsh	Betty Arnold (1939–41)
Laura Martin	Gail Henshaw (1940–41)
Ellis Smith	Raymond Edward Johnson (1937–39)
	Sam Wanamaker (1939–40)
	Phil Dakin (1940)
	Marvin Miller (1940–42)
	Karl Weber (1942)
Dr. Jonathan MacNeill	Sidney Breese (1943–46)
Nina Lawrence Chadwick	Lois Zarley (1943–46)
	Barbara Luddy (1946)
Tim Lawrence	Les Mitchell (1943)
	Rye Billsbury (1943–46)
Claire Marshall Lawrence	Eloise Kummer (1943–46)
	Sharon Grainger (1946)
Lucille Marshall	Constance Crowder (1945–46)
Dr. Richard Gaylord	John Barclay (1944–46)
Mrs. Gaylord	Helen Buell (1944–46)
Peggy Gaylord	Jane Webb (1944–46)
Dwight Lamont	Maurice Copeland (1945–46)
Rev. Bill Brown	Jerry Walters (1945–46)
Rev. Frank Tuttle	Phillip Lord (1945)
Abigail Peck	Henrietta Tedro (1945–46)

Mrs. Hanson	Alma Platts (1945)
Marjorie Vance	Jean Mowry (1945)
Court Davis	Duke Watson (1946)
Dr. Charles Matthews	Hugh Studebaker (1947–49)
Julie Collins	Mary Lansing (1946–47)
Roger Collins	Sam Edwards (1946)
Frank Collins	Willis Bouchey (1947)
Phyllis Gordon	Sharon Grainger (1944–46)
Peter Manno	Michael Romano (1937; 1944–46)
Dr. Mary Leland	Anne Seymour (1948–51)
Rev. Dr. Paul Keeler	Bernard Lenrow (1949–50)
	Bill Smith (1950–52)
Ray Brandon	Don Briggs (1946–47)
	Willard Waterman (1947–49)
	Staats Cotsworth (1949–50)
	Donald Briggs (1950–51)
Charlotte Wilson Brandon	Gertrude Warner (1947)
	Betty Lou Gerson (1947–48)
	Lesley Woods (1949–51)
Ross Boling	Karl Weber (1950–51)
Ted White	Arnold Moss (1948–49)
	Bert Cowlan (1949–50)
	James Monks (1950)
Meta Bauer White	Gloria Blondell (1948)
	Dorothy Lovett (1948–49)
	Jone Allison (1949–52)
Trudy Bauer	Laurette Fillbrandt (1948)
	Charlotte Holland (1949–51)
Bill Bauer	Lyle Sudrow (1948–52)
Bertha Miller Bauer	Ann Shepherd (1949–50)
	Charita Bauer (1950–52)
Papa Bauer	Theodore von Eltz (1948–49)
	Theo Goetz (1949–52)
Mama Bauer	Gloria Brandt (1948–49)
	Adelaide Klein (1949)
Joe Roberts	Larry Haines (1950–51)
	Herb Nelson (1951–52)
Kathy Roberts	Susan Douglas (1950–52)
Joey Roberts	Tarry Green (1950–52)

Radio Production Credits

Creator-writer: Irna Phillips

Producers: David Lesan, Joe Ainley, Carl Wester

Directors: Gordon Hughes, Joe Ainley, Charles Urquhart, Harry Bubeck,
    Howard Keegan, Ted MacMurray

Sound Effects: Ralph Cummings, Hamilton O'Hara

Announcers: Hugh Downs, Ed Prentiss, Herb Allen, Bud Collyer

Organist: Bernice Yanacek, Rosa Rio

Theme: *Aphrodite*
    "Variations on Romance from Wieniaswski's Violin Concerto, #2 in D
    Minor"

Television Cast 1952–87

Bert Bauer	Charita Bauer (1952–84)
Bill Bauer	Lyle Sudrow (1952–59)
	Ed Bryce (1959–63; 1965–69; 1977–78; 1983)
	Eugene Smith (1964)
Papa Bauer	Theo Goetz (1952–72)
Mike Bauer	Glenn Walken (1954–56)
	Michael Allen (1959–62)
	Paul Prokopf (1962–63)
	Gary Pillar (Carpenter) (1963–66)
	Robert Pickering (1968)
	Don Stewart (1968–84)
Dr. Ed Bauer	Pat Collins (1959–61)
	Robert Gentry (1966–69)
	Mart Hulswit (1969–81)
	Peter Simon (1981–84; 1986–)
	Richard Van Vleet (1984–86)

Meta Roberts Banning

Joe Roberts
Kathy Roberts Holden
Joey Roberts

Trudy Bauer

Elsie Miller Franklin
Rev. Dr. Paul Keeler

Sid Harper
Gloria LaRue Harper
Mac
Dr. Dick Grant
Laura Grant

Richard Grant
Marie Wallace Grant

Mrs. Laurey

Dr. Jim Kelly
Lila Taylor Kelly

Dr. John Brooks
Dr. Bart Thompson
Dan Peters
Peggy Regan
Richard Hanley, D.A.
Dr. Baird
Janet Johnson, R.N.

Mark Holden
Alice Holden

Robin Lang Fletcher

Jone Allison (1952)
Ellen Demming (1953–74)
Herb Nelson (1952–55)
Susan Douglas (1952–58)
Tarry Green (1952–53)
Richard Holland (1953)
Helen Wagner (1952)
Lisa Howard (1957–58)
Ethel Remey (1956–57)
Ed Begley (1952)
Melville Ruick (1952–54)
Philip Sterling (1952–54)
Anne Burr (1952–54)
Arnold Robertson (1953)
James Lipton (1952–62)
Katherine Anderson (1953)
Alice Yourman (1953–62)
Ed Prentiss (1953)
Joyce Holden (1954)
Lynne Rogers (1955–62)
Lois Wilson (1954–55)
Virginia Payne (1956)
Paul Potter (1954–55)
Nancy Wickwire (1954–55)
Teri Keane (1957)
Charles Baxter (1954)
Barry Thomson (1954)
Paul Ballantyne (1954)
Patricia Wheel (1954)
Mandel Kramer (1953)
Peter Cappell (1953–55)
Ruth Warrick (1953–54)
Lois Wheeler (1954–58)
Whitfield Connor (1955–59)
Sandy Dennis (1956)
Diane Gentner (1956–58)
Lin Pierson (1958–60)
Zina Bethune (1956–58)
Judy Robinson (1959–60)

Robin Lang Fletcher (cont'd)	Abigail Kellogg (1960–61)
	Nancy Malone (1961–63)
	Ellen Weston (1963–64)
	Gillian Spencer (1964–67)
Fred Fletcher	John Gibson (1958)
Dr. Paul Fletcher	Michael Kane (1956)
	Bernard Grant (1956–70)
Anne Benedict Fletcher	Joan Gray (1956–62)
	Elizabeth Hubbard (1962)
Henry Benedict	John Gibson (1959–62)
	John Boruff (1962–66)
	Paul McGrath (1967)
	Lester Rawlins (1967)
Helene Benedict	Kay Campbell (1957–64)
Dr. Bruce Banning	Les Damon (1956–60)
	Barnard Hughes (1961–66)
	Sydney Walker (1970–71)
	William Roerick (1974)
Ruth Jannings Holden	Irja Jensen (1958)
	Louise Platt (1958–59)
	Virginia Dwyer (1959–60)
Karl Jannings	Richard Morse (1959–60)
Marian Winters	Katherine Meskill (1957)
Edna Marsh	Zamah Cunningham (1957)
Joe Turino	Joseph Campanella (1959–60)
Amy Sinclair	Joanne Linville (1959)
	Connie Lembcke (1960)
Philip Collins	Carson Woods (1960–61)
Alex Bowden	Ernest Graves (1960–66)
Doris Crandall	Barbara Becker (1961–62)
George Hayes	Philip Sterling (1963–68)
Jane Fletcher Hayes	Pamela King (1961–63)
	Chase Crosley (1963–68)
Dr. John Fletcher	Sheldon Golomb (1962)
	Donald Melvin (1963–64)
	Daniel Fortas (1965)
	Don Scardino (1965–67)
	Erik Howell (1967–71)
Dr. Peter Nelson	Gene Rupert (1963–64)

Julie Conrad Bauer	Sandra Smith (1962–65)
Hope Bauer	Jennifer Kirschner (1964–65)
	Paula Schwartz (1968)
	Elissa Leeds (1968–73)
	Tisch Raye (1975–76)
	Robin Mattson (1976–77)
	Katherine Justice (1977)
	Elvera Roussel (1979–83)
Dr. Stephen Jackson	Stefan Schnabel (1965–81)
Leslie Jackson Bauer	Lynne Adams (1966–71; 1973–76)
	Kathryn Hays (1971)
	Barbara Rodell (1971–73)
Peggy Scott Thorpe	Fran Myers (1965–79)
Ben Scott	Bernard Kates (1965–68)
Maggie Scott	June Graham (1965–68)
Jason Weber	Marc O'Daniels (1965–66)
Lt. Carl Wyatt	Gerald S. O'Loughlin (1965)
Andrew Murray	Dana Elcar (1965)
Mrs. Matson	Fran Bennett (1965–66)
Carol	Louise Stubbs (1965–66)
Jack Haskell	Paul Larson (1966)
Dr. Jim Frazier	Billy Dee Williams (1966)
	James Earl Jones (1966)
Martha Frazier	Cicely Tyson (1966)
	Ruby Dee (1967)
Dr. Sara McIntyre	Patricia Roe (1967)
	Jill Andre (1967–68)
	Millette Alexander (1969–82)
Dr. Joe Werner	Ben Hayes (1966–67)
	Ed Zimmermann (1967–72)
	Berkeley Harris (1972)
	Anthony Call (1972–76)
Tim (T.J.) Werner	T.J. Hargrave (1974–76)
	Kevin Bacon (1980–81)
	Christopher Marcantel (1981)
	Nigel Reed (1981–82)
Charlotte Waring Bauer	Victoria Wyndham (1967–70)
	Melinda Fee (1970–73)

Lee Gantry	Ray Fulmer (1969–71)
Miss Mildred Foss	Jan Sterling (1969–70)
Marty Dillman	Robert Lawson (1968)
	Christopher Wines (1969)
Claudia Dillman	Grace Matthews (1968–69)
Dr. Gavin Hamilton	Paul McGrath (1968)
Sgt. DeMarco	Michael Mikler (1969)
Lt. Wally Campbell	Alexander Courtney (1969)
	Jack Ryland (1969)
Lt. Pete Stassen	Karl Light (1969)
Judy Stassen	Ruth Manning (1969)
Ira Newton	Sorrell Booke (1969)
	Larry Gates (1972)
Flip Malone	Paul Carpinelli (1969)
Deborah Mehren	Olivia Cole (1969–71)
Gil Mehren	David Pendleton (1970–71)
	James A. Preston (1971)
Peter Wexler	Leon Russom (1969)
	Michael Durrell (1969–71)
Maggie Wexler	Margaret Impert (1969)
Marion McHenry, R.N.	Marion Lauer (1969–72)
Nurse Stanhope	Donna Oddams (1969)
Tyler Meade	Paul Collins (1969–70)
Dusty McGuire	Jamie Donnelly (1969–70)
Tom Halverson	Chris Sarandon (1969–70)
Judge Evan Kruger	Hansford Rowe (1969)
Kate Pearson	Jane Farnol (1970)
Lady Kimball	Anita Dangler (1970)
Sir Clayton Olds	Myles Easton (1970)
Dinah Buckley	Courtney Sherman (1970–71)
Christy Rogers	Ariane Munker (1970–71)
Billy Fletcher	James Long (1970–73)
	Matthew Schlossberg (1973)
	Shane Nickerson (1973–76)
	Dai Stockton (1976)
Kit Vested	Nancy Addison (1970–74)
David Vested	Peter D. Greene (1970–71)
	Dan Hamilton (1971)

Stanley Norris	Michael Higgins (1970)
	William Smithers (1971)
Barbara Norris Thorpe	Augusta Dabney (1970)
	Barbara Berjer (1971–81)
Andrew Norris	Barney McFadden (1975)
	Ted LePlat (1980–81)
Holly Norris	Lynn Deerfield (1970–76)
	Maureen Garrett (1976–80)
Ken Norris	Roger Newman (1970–75)
Janet Mason Norris	Caroline McWilliams (1969–75)
Ellen Mason	Jeanne Arnold (1969–73)
Grove Mason	Vince O'Brien (1969–70)
Roger Thorpe	Michael Zaslow (1971–80)
Adam Thorpe	Robert Gerringer (1972)
	Robert Milli (1972–81)
Christina Thorpe	Gina Foy (1975–78)
	Cheryl Lynn Brown (1979–80)
Linell Conway	Christina Pickles (1970–72)
Marion Conway	Lois Holmes (1971)
	Kate Harrington (1971–72)
Karen Martin	Tudi Wiggins (1971–72)
Betty Eiler	Madeleine Sherwood (1971–72)
Charles Eiler	Graham Jarvis (1971–72)
Rita Putnam	Anne Shaler (1972)
Emma Earnest	Agnes Young (1972–73)
Leona Herbert	Rosetta LeNoire (1972)
Camilla Crawford	Penelope Windust (1972)
Capt. Jim Swanson	Lee Richardson (1972)
Dr. Dick Carey	Paul Nesbit (1972)
	Roger Morden (1972–73)
Victoria Ballenger	Carol Teitel (1973–74)
Alex	Tom Klunis (1974)
Dr. Wilson Frost	Jack Betts (1973–74)
Audrey Mills	Louise Troy (1974)
Roy Mills	Josef Sommer (1974)
Dr. Bertrand Mandel	Fred J. Scollay (1974)
Mrs. Hoffman	Lilia Skala (1974)
Dr. Carl Richards	Wayne Tippit (1974)

Dr. Barry Flannery   Robert Phelps (1974)

Dr. Harold Eberhart   Jordan Charney (1974)

Pam Chandler   Maureen Silliman (1974–76)

Dr. Tim Ryan   Jordan Clarke (1974–76)

Chad Richards   Everett McGill (1975–76)

Ann Jeffers   Maureen Mooney (1975–79)

Spence Jeffers   John Ramsey (1976)

Alex McDaniels   Keith Charles (1976)

Viola Stapleton   Sudie Bond (1975)

     Kate Wilkinson (1975–81)

Rita Stapleton Bauer   Leonore Kasdorf (1975–81)

Eve Stapleton McFarren   Janet Grey (1976–83)

Ben McFarren   Stephen Yates (1976–82)

Jerry McFarren   Peter Jensen (1976)

     Mark Travis (1977)

Malcolm Granger   Ed Seamon (1976)

Georgene Granger   Delphi Harrington (1977)

Raymond Shafer   Keith Aldrich (1977)

Dr. Emmet Scott   Kenneth Harvey (1976)

     Frank Latimore (1976–79)

     Peter Turgeon (1981)

Dr. Justin Marler   Tom O'Rourke (1976–83)

Jackie Marler   Cindy Pickett (1976–80)

     Carrie Mowery (1980–82)

Lainie Marler Bowden   Kathleen Kellaigh (1979–80)

Ross Marler   Jerry verDorn (1979–)

Alan Spaulding   Christopher Bernau (1977–84; 1986–)

Elizabeth Spaulding   Lezlie Dalton (1977–81)

Phillip Spaulding   Jarrod Ross (1977–81)

     Grant Aleksander (1982–84)

     John Bolger (1985–)

Frederick (Rick) Bauer   Albert Zungallo (1970–71)

     Gary Hannoch (1972–76)

     Robbie Berridge (1976–78)

     Phil MacGregor (1982–83)

     Michael O'Leary (1983–)

Hillary Kincaid Bauer   Linda McCullough (1977–78)

     Marsha Clark (1978–84)

Simone Kincaid	Laryssa Lauret (1977–78)
Dean Blackford	Gordon Rigsby (1977–79)
Max Chapman	Ben Hammer (1978)
Dr. Peter Chapman	Curt Dawson (1978–80)
Dr. Mark Hamilton	Burton Cooper (1978–79)
Katie Parker	Denise Pence (1977–85)
Floyd Parker	Tom Nielsen (1979–85)
Brandy Shellooe	Sandy Faison (1977)
	JoBeth Williams (1977–81)
Diane Ballard	Sofia Landon (1977–81)
Brandon Spaulding	David Thomas (1979)
	John Wardwell (1983)
	Keith Charles (1984)
Lucille Wexler	Rita Lloyd (1978–80)
Amanda Wexler Spaulding	Kathleen Cullen (1978–83)
Gordon Middleton	Marcus Smythe (1978–79)
Carmen Monvales	Julie Carmen (1978)
	Blanca Camacho (1978–80)
Lt. Larry Wyatt	Joe Ponazecki (1979–82)
Clarence Bailey	Philip Bosco (1979)
	Lawrence Weber (1982–85)
Whitney Foxton	Joseph Maher (1978)
Dr. Gonzalo Moreno	Gonzalo Madurga (1978)
Maya Waterman	Sands Hall (1978)
Linette Waterman	Eileen Dietz (1978)
Dr. Waterman	Maurice Copeland (1978)
Gladys Shields	Louise Troy (1978)
Josh McPhee	Ben Thomas (1979)
Scott Lacey	David Leary (1979)
Dr. Margaret Sedwick	Margaret Gwenver (1979–)
Sylvia Moreno	Feiga Martinez (1979)
Clara Jones	Anna Maria Hosford (1979)
Dr. Ruth Creighton	Roni Dengel (1979)
Neil Blake	Patrick Horgan (1979–80)
Dr. Greg Fairbanks	David Greenan (1979–80)
Dr. Paul LaCrosse	Jacques Roux (1979–80)
Dr. Renee DuBois	Deborah May (1979–80)
Ivy Pierce	Deborah May (1982–83)

Dr. Ingrid Fischer — Tania Elg (1980)
Carter Bowden — Alan Austin (1980)
Emily, Spaulding maid — Elizabeth Swain (1980–82)
Darren Patterson — John Rockwell (1980)
Dr. Erik Bernhoff — Frederick Rolf (1980)
Maggie O'Byrne — Shelia Coonan (1980–81)
Jennifer Richards — Geraldine Court (1980–83)
Morgan Richards Nelson — Kristen Vigard (1980–81)
Jennifer Cook (1981–83)
Kelly Nelson — John Wesley Shipp (1980–84)
Nola Reardon Chamberlain — Lisa Brown (1980–85)
Bea Reardon — Lee Lawson (1980–   )
Tony Reardon — Gregory Beecroft (1981–85)
Maureen Reardon Bauer — Ellen Dolan (1982–86)
Ellen Parker (1986–   )
Dr. Jim Reardon — Michael Woods (1983–85)
Henry Chamberlain — William Roerick (1980–   )
Vanessa Chamberlain Lewis — Maeve Kinkead (1980–   )
Anna Stuart (1980–81)
Quinton McCord Chamberlain — Michael Tylo (1981–85)
Violet Renfield — Beulah Garrick (1981–83)
Logan Stafford — Richard Hamilton (1980–81)
Chet Stafford — Bill Herndon (1980–81)
Joe Bradley — Michael J. Stark (1980–81)
Duke Lafferty — Gary Phillips (1980)
Derek Colby — Harley Venton (1981–82)
Gracie Middleton — Lori Shelle (1981–83)
Trudy Wilson — Amy Steel (1980–81)
Lesley Ann Monroe — Carolyn Ann Clarke (1981–84)
Carrie Todd — Jane Elliot (1981–82)
Mark Evans — Mark Pinter (1981–83)
Mona Enright — Leslie O'Hara (1982–83)
Bryan Lister — Richard Clarke (1982–83)
Silas Crocker — Benjamin Hendrickson (1981–83)
Helena Manzini — Rose Alaio (1981–83)
Kirk Winters — James Horan (1981)
Blanche Bouvier — Jennifer Leak (1981)
Dr. Frank Nelson — Keith Charles (1981)

Wayne Jennings	Roger Baron (1981)
Lucien Goff	Andreas Katsulas (1982)
Ron Kennedy	Matthew Barry (1982)
Joan Bennett	Herself (1982)
Susanna Hayden	Lori Putnam (1983)
Eddie	Edward Vilella (1983)
Fritz	Bill Britton (1982)
Gunther Lugosi	George Kappaz (1982)
Jamie Loomis	Alan Coates (1982)
Paulie Amato	Michael Madeiros (1982)
Clay Tynan	Giancarlo Esposito (1982–83)
Helen Tynan	Micki Grant (1982–84)
Martin Bruner	Clement Fowler (1983)
Annabelle Sims Reardon	Harley Kozak (1983–85)
Commander Eli Sims	Stephen Joyce (1983)
Agatha Dobson	Elizabeth MacRae (1983)
Dr. Gwen Harding	Elizabeth Allen (1983)
H.B. Lewis	Larry Gates (1983–)
Trish Lewis	Rebecca Hollen (1981–85)
Josh Lewis	Robert Newman (1981–84; 1986–)
Reva Shayne Lewis	Kim Zimmer (1983–)
Billy Lewis	Jordan Clarke (1983–)
Mindy Lewis	Krista Tesreau (1983–)
Beth Raines	Judi Evans (1983–86)
Lillian Raines	Tina Sloan (1983–)
Bradley Raines	James Rebhorn (1983–85)
Nick	Rex Everhart (1983–84)
Dr. Claire Ramsey	Susan Pratt (1983–)
Dr. Louie Darnell	Eric Brooks (1983–)
Warren Andrews	Warren Burton (1983–)
Alexandra Spaulding	Beverlee McKinsey (1984–)
Lujack (Brandon Luvonaczek)	Vincent Irizarry (1983–85)
Darcy Dekker	Robin V. Johnson (1984)
Martin (I.Q.) Wilson	Jaison Walker (1984–85)
Pretty Boy	David Rod Coury (1984)
Gina Daniels	Annabelle Gurwitch (1984–85)
Fletcher Reade	Charles Jay Hammer (1984–)
Lola Fontaine	Megan McTavish (1983–84)

Wayne De Vargas
Jane Hogan
Susan Piper
Emma Witherspoon
Zamana
Sharina
Victoria
Jonathan Brooks
Roz Sharp
Muffy Baxter
India von Halkein
Roxie Shayne
Hawk Shayne
Sally Gleason
Kyle Sampson
David Preston
Suzette Saxon
Jackson Freemont
Andy Ferris
Nancy Ferris
Johnny "Dub" Taylor
Lionel Harris
Lt. Jeff Saunders
Nurse Jodie
Kurt Corday
Charlotte Wheaton
Alicia Rohmer
Maeve Stoddard
Calla Matthews
Jesse Matthews
Simon Hall
Cain Harris
Baron Leo von Halkein
Sophia Breitner
Dorie Smith
Dinah Morgan
Johnny Bauer
Julia Stoddard

Peter Brouwer (1984)
Mary Pat Gleason (1984–85)
Carrie Nye (1984)
Maureen O'Sullivan (1984)
Adolph Caesar (1984)
Janet League (1984)
Kim Hamilton (1984)
Damion Scheller (1984–85)
Carolyn Byrd (1984)
Bradley Bliss (1984)
Mary Kay Adams (1984–   )
Kristi Ferrell (1984–   )
Gil Rogers (1985–   )
Patricia Barry (1984–   )
Larkin Malloy (1984–   )
John Martinuzzi (1984–85)
Frances Fisher (1985)
Michael Wilding, Jr. (1985–   )
Victor Slezak (1984–85)
J. Smith-Cameron (1984–85)
Maarko Maglich (1984–85)
Jack White (1984–   )
David Little (1984–85)
Alice Oakes (1985–   )
Mark Lewis (1985–86)
Barbara Garrick (1985)
Cynthia Dozier (1985)
Leslie Denniston (1985–   )
Lisby Larson (1985–   )
Rebecca Staab (1985–   )
Shawn Thompson (1985–   )
Jerry Lanning (1986)
George Guidall (1986)
Lizabeth Pritchett (1986)
Kimi Parks (1986–   )
Jennifer Gatti (1986–   )
James Goodwin (1986–   )
Meg Mundy (1986)

Pat Beagle   Arthur E. Jones (1985–   )
Wally Bacon   Jack Armstrong (1985)
                                  Michael Conforti (1986–   )
Dick Sexton   Patrick James Clarke (1986–   )
Grace Cummings   Teresa Wright (1986)
Dr. Mark Jarrett   Keir Dullea (1986)

Television Production Credits

Creator: Irna Phillips

Production Company: Compton Advertising Inc., for Procter & Gamble Productions

Executive Producers: Lucy Ferri Rittenberg, Allen Potter, Gail Kobe, Joe Willmore

Producers: David Lesan, Richard Dunn, Peter Andrews, Harry Eggart, Charlotte Savitz, Leslie Kwartin, Joe Willmore, Robert Calhoun, John P. Whitesell II, Robert D. Kochman, Linda Barker Laundra, Hope Harmel Smith

Headwriters: Irna Phillips; Agnes Nixon; David Lesan and Julian Funt; Theodore and Mathilde Ferro; John Boruff; James Lipton; Gabrielle Upton; Jane and Ira Avery; Robert Soderberg and Edith Sommer; James Gentile; Robert Cenedella; Bridget and Jerome Dobson; Douglas Marland; Pat Falken Smith; L. Virginia Browne; Richard Culliton; Pamela Long Hammer; Jeff Ryder; Mary Ryan Munisteri; Sheri Anderson

Associate Writers: Agnes Nixon, William J. Bell, David Lesan, Kathryn McCabe, Don Wallace, J.J. Matthew (Don Hastings), John Vlahos, Leonard Kantor, Doris Frankel, Linda Grover, Frances Rickett, Joyce Perry, Jean Rouverol, Nancy Ford, Rocci Chatfield, Peggy O'Shea, Robert White, Phyllis White, Charles diZenzo, Patricia diZenzo, Robert Dwyer, Nancy Franklin, Frank Salisbury, Harding Lemay, Patrick Mulcahey, Gene Palumbo, Minnie Warburton, Carey Wilber, Carolyn DeMoney Culliton, Charles Jay Hammer, Addie Walsh, Judith Donato, John Kuntz, Christopher Whitesell, Samuel D. Ratcliffe, Robin Amos, Stephanie Braxton,

Stephen Demorest, Trent Jones, Michelle Poteet-Lisanti, N. Gail Lawrence, Pete T. Rich, Megan McTavish, Elaine Potwardoski, Emily Squires, Edward Parone, Mary Pat Gleason, Martha Nochimson, Ellen Barrett

Directors: Ted Corday, Walter Gorman, Jack Wood, Gray Delmar, John Neukum, Leonard Valenta, Nick Havinga, John Litvack, Jeff Bleckner, Peter Miner, John Sedwick, Allen Fristoe, Harry Eggart, Lynwood King, John Pasquin, Michael Gliona, Bruce Barry, Jill Mitwell, John P. Whitesell II, Irene M. Pace, Dan Smith, Matthew Diamond, Scott McKinsey, Jo Ann Rivituso, Joanne Sedwick

Organists: Bert Buhrman, John Gart, Charles Paul

Musical Directors: Charles Paul, Elliot Lawrence Productions

Address for fan mail:
    Guiding Light
    c/o CBS-TV
    51 West 52nd Street
    New York, NY 10019

Fan Club: Guiding Light Fan Club
    Christopher S. Mullen
    2855 Stevens Street
    Oceanside, NY 11572

Index

Note: Italic numbers designate pages where photos appear.

About the Author

Christopher Schemering is the author of *The Soap Opera Encyclopedia*, the first book to provide information on every network daytime and prime-time soap opera ever broadcast on television. He has written a syndicated column on the soaps, and has had articles on television and film published in *The New Republic, USA Today, The Chicago Tribune, Soap Opera Digest*, and many other publications. He is a regular contributor to *The Washington Post Book World*, specializing in reviewing fiction and books on show business. He lives in Washington, D.C.